ON THE ROCKS WITH

JACK
KNOX

ON THE ROCKS WITH

JACK KNOX

ISLANDERS I WILL NEVER FORGET

H
HERITAGE

VICTORIA · VANCOUVER · CALGARY

To my parents.

Heritage House Publishing Company Ltd.
heritagehouse.ca

Cataloguing information available from Library and Archives Canada

978-1-77203-266-6 (pbk)
978-1-77203-267-3 (epub)

Edited by Merrie-Ellen Wilcox
Proofread by Jesmine Cham
Cover and interior design and illustration by Jacqui Thomas
All interior photographs are courtesy of the Victoria *Times Colonist*.

The interior of this book was produced on 100% post-consumer recycled
paper, processed chlorine free, and printed with vegetable-based inks.

We acknowledge the financial support of the Government of Canada through
the Canada Book Fund (CBF) and the Canada Council for the Arts, and the
Province of British Columbia through the British Columbia Arts Council
and the Book Publishing Tax Credit.

22 21 20 19 18 1 2 3 4 5

Printed in Canada

contents

introduction

THIS IS NOT a humour book.

I say this because my previous books, *Hard Knox* and *Opportunity Knox*, fell in that category, so it might be natural for you to assume this one would, too. I would hate for you to plough into these pages expecting to double over in a paroxysm of choking-on-your-gum laughter (or, more likely, to twitch your lips in mild amusement) only to be disappointed. So, no, while *On the Rocks* does have some laughs in it, it is not primarily a humour book.

Nor is this a book about The News and The Important Issues of the Day. I have spent the past thirty years at Victoria's *Times Colonist* newspaper dealing with politics and pipelines, the economy and the environment, courts and crime, social issues, transportation, terrorism, and all the other weighty staples of purple-faced punditry—but you won't read about them here. (I will die contented if I never have to write another word about sewage treatment.)

No, this book is about people.

Not famous people, either, but ordinary—make that extraordinary—people you probably have never heard of but whose stories are remarkable nonetheless. They're the ones

I stumbled across in a career spent poking my nose around Vancouver Island.

There's a guy who used to go for milk and cookies at Adolf Hitler's house when his aunt was Hitler's girlfriend. There's a man who could only converse in his first language in his dreams, because he was the last person on earth to speak it. There's another who lived through the horror of the atomic bomb at Nagasaki, only to emerge as one of the most good-natured, good-hearted people you could ever find.

There's Barry Campbell, king of the beachcombers, in Tofino, and Pat Carney, queen of the coast, on Saturna Island. There's a man who faked the last name in the phone book, another who roller skated across Canada, and a woman who used to fire a machine gun into the bush to keep bandits at bay.

There's a couple who spent four and a half months rowing across the Atlantic Ocean together, just the two of them in a tiny boat, another couple who only wanted to spend their entire lives together, just the two of them alone in a lighthouse, and another couple who stayed behind on Nootka Island, just the two of them in their ancestral home of four thousand years, after everyone else moved away half a century ago.

There are Kosovar and Vietnamese refugees, a tiny immigrant single mom who carved out a life in a tiny sandwich shop, and a legendary street cop. There's a long section dedicated to Second World War veterans whose stories might have disappeared had they not agreed (often reluctantly) to share them: D-Day sailors who swiped an American jeep, survivors of the hell at Dieppe, a prisoner of war who would surreptitiously shake escape-tunnel dirt from pouches hidden in his clothing.

I have plunked in a few old columns whole, pretty much the way they appeared when first published in the newspaper.

Other chapters pull together stories I have followed for decades, like the struggle of Alert Bay's Kwakwa̱ka̱'wakw people to recover, piece by piece, cultural treasures scattered around the world after a potlatch was raided a century ago. That's one of the tales the photographer Debra Brash and I came across when, over the course of several years, we explored the back roads and isolated places for a series called "The Other Island."

We began that series with a simple idea, the notion that there is a whole other Vancouver Island out there that most of us never see, the Land Beyond Starbucks, where people's lives are so different from those in the paved and high-rised cities.

This book picks up on that theme, except instead of being limited to stories of people you have never seen, it also tells the tales of those you walk past on the sidewalk every day. People you don't know, but whose hidden stories make you wish you did.

yuquot

CAPTAIN COOK DROPPED anchor in their kitchen. Spain and Britain came to the brink of war in their front yard. When they sit on their weather-worn porch, sipping their morning coffee, they gaze at the bay where the crew of the *Boston* was wiped out, where John R. Jewitt was taken into slavery two hundred years ago.

But all that was recent history, relatively speaking. For Terry and Ray Williams, the roots go much deeper. Four thousand years or more.

It's easy to lose the sense of time in Yuquot, way off on the edge of Nootka Island, a two-hour boat ride from the nearest town.

Terry and Ray are the last Indigenous people to spend their lives here year-round, following a path that is in many ways closer to that of their ancestors than of the Big Mac–munching, Netflix-binging mainstream world.

They still know the old language and gather and eat what nature provides in a place with no roads, no power lines, and little outside contact. A fallen totem pole lies rotting just steps from their home.

The history books call this Friendly Cove, the Birthplace of BC, where Indigenous and European cultures first came

4

into contact. The Spanish traded here in 1774 but didn't get off their ship, the *Santiago*. Captain James Cook came ashore in 1778, mistaking the inhabitants' call of "*itchme nutka, itchme nutka*" for the name of the place, which he wrote as "Nootka."

They were actually calling "come around," beckoning him to Yuquot—"Where the winds blow from many directions"— the Mowachaht people's summer home, a once-thriving community of 1,500 people and twenty longhouses.

The people are gone now. So are the longhouses, though Ray and Terry can remember a couple of them from their childhood. The longhouses were replaced by a church, a light station, a couple of wooden buildings, a dock. The wind still blows, ruffling the grass around the foundations of a long-gone school, bending the ferns in the overgrown cemetery, where headstones dating back to the First World War peek out at the open Pacific Ocean. But these are all modern trappings, having little to do with the whaling people who existed here before.

Maybe it's all the history, Indigenous and European both. Maybe it's the ghostly silence, the remoteness. Whatever— Yuquot feels steeped in the past. Eerie.

"You can sense all those years," says Terry. "You can really feel it . . . All this really happened, right here."

Ray senses it, too. "We know that we're protected. Our ancestors take care of us."

Terry, seventy-four, has been here all her life. Ray, seventy-seven, was born in Port Alberni, but came to Yuquot as a baby. When the Mowachaht/Muchalaht band moved to Gold River to find work in the 1960s, they stayed behind.

"I was born and raised here," Terry shrugged in explanation on the day I first met her in 2003. "I loved this place . . . I had a really happy childhood here. I loved every minute of it."

She tried living in Gold River for a couple of months in 1967. "I didn't like it."

What keeps them in Yuquot, far from the land of traffic jams, Costco, and Starbucks drive-throughs?

"Peace and quiet," says Ray. "We live off the ocean, live off the land, which is special to us."

There's an old expression on the West Coast: "When it's low tide, our table is set." They eat *k'uc'im*, or mussels, and *hay'istup*, the chitons that they peel off rocks. They like *t'uc'up*—sea urchins—the green ones, the ones called raspberries for their colour and size, or the big purple guys. (It's said that eating too many purple *t'uc'up* will send you into a deep sleep.) All are eaten raw.

Other foods come with the seasons. February and March are the months for herring. Their roe is gathered from kelp, or from hemlock boughs laid on the water. Then the halibut come offshore, along with the ling cod and red snapper. The sockeye salmon run from May through July. Chinook arrive next, then chum. The coho are last to spawn.

A generator provides power, but the house is heated with wood. Terry used a washboard until getting a washing machine in 1993. "A lot of people living in town are dependent on everything electric—microwaves, toasters," she says. "It makes you lazy."

On the day we met, Ray and Terry were taking a break in the afternoon sun. They had been peeling cedar bark for the last three days. Their son, carver Sanford Williams, uses it in his masks. They pick swamp grass for basket-weaving, too.

While they spoke, their four-year-old granddaughter played at their feet, ostensibly helping granddad fix an outboard motor. Her English name is Olivia, her native name

K'wak'wat, or sea otter. They were teaching her bits of the Mowachaht dialect of the Nuu-chah-nulth language.

"What are you doing?" she asked. It sounded like "Ah-kin-a-puck."

Olivia had just turned nineteen when I last spoke to Ray, at the beginning of 2018. She lived in Vancouver but visited Nootka Island now and then. Her place at Yuquot had been taken by the Williams's six-year-old great-grandson and a couple of other family members. Son Sanford, who lives in the Fraser Valley, spends part of each summer there, finding it an inspiring place to do his carving—masks, paddles, totems, doors, bentwood boxes.

"I like the ocean," Sanford says. "I like the quietness of it." His own story, including his traumatizing childhood at BC's last residential school, was told in the 2016 book *Eagle in the Owl's Nest*, by his wife, Marlana Williams.

Ray went to the Christie residential school near Tofino, too, in 1946. It was there that he forgot his language, only to regain it after marrying Terry in 1962. "I never lost it," Terry says. They converse in Mowachaht when linguistically challenged visitors aren't around.

They remain rooted, content. "We have never lived in an apartment in our lives," says Ray one day in early 2018. "If we leave here, we'll just die quicker." Yuquot is, in fact, where they will stay to the end, he says. It's a peaceful life. "We mostly just sit, look out the window, have coffee."

The lighthouse is clearly visible, a city block away, but Ray and Terry don't mix much with the lightkeepers. Nothing personal. It's just the way they are. They go into Gold River maybe three times during the summer, and even less in winter, when travel in an open speedboat isn't terribly appealing.

It can be a real shock when they do step into the paved part of the world. In 2003, their eyes widened at the memory of a 1993 trip to New York, a journey made at the behest of some documentary filmmakers. "It really blew our mind," says Ray. "The tall buildings! The bridges across the river!"

The top of the Empire State Building proved too much. "I froze up there. I couldn't move," Terry says. Ray nods in agreement: "We kissed the ground when we got back down."

Not that they're totally cut off from what passes for civilization. Sanford got them a satellite dish and television as the twenty-first century began. Ray soon found himself watching the Aboriginal Peoples Television Network, baseball at the end of the season, and the news. ("It's always bad news, but it's different bad news.") The old shows were new to them: *The Love Boat, I Love Lucy.* Terry likes *Three's Company.* "It makes me laugh," Ray says.

Today they're even more in tune with the modern world. They have a telephone now, even a computer.

They also see a steady stream of people in the summer, at least in short bursts. The *Uchuck III,* a 1942 minesweeper converted to carry passengers and freight, chugs up from Gold River three times a week in tourist season, giving visitors a couple of hours ashore. For those who want to stay longer, the band rents campsites and cabins in the woods. Sailboats, float planes, and kayaks drop by.

Yuquot is also at the end of the increasingly busy Nootka Trail. The Williamses remember when it was only a handful of local loggers who would try the thirty-seven-kilometre slog down the wild west coast of the island. Now there's a steady stream doing the trek, which typically takes four to eight days after being flown by float plane to the trail's northern terminus.

The Williamses are at ease with strangers, though Ray feels a responsibility to keep an eye on things. Visitors long treated Yuquot as a public souvenir trove to be plundered, trying to cart away everything from the arms from a totem pole to old-fashioned seine blocks from the beach. Someone even took off with the bell from the church, way back when.

It used to be common for Indigenous people to be buried with treasured possessions—masks, blankets—placed on their resting places. By the dawn of this century, the last evidence of that in the Yuquot cemetery was a rusted old sewing machine sitting on a grave. The rest of the treasures were stolen long ago. The thievery got so bad that Chief Ambrose Maquinna temporarily barred non–band members from the property in the 1960s.

Visitors are welcome again, though they can expect to help pay for the boardwalk and other upkeep: there's a fee for Nootka Trail hikers and a landing charge for those who come off the dock after disembarking from the *Uchuck* or alighting from a float plane (it's forty minutes by air from Gold River).

Caretakers from the Mowachaht/Muchalaht First Nation summer at Yuquot, and guides offer tours of the area: here are the old gathering places, here's where Cook landed, here's what's left of Fort San Miguel, the only fort the Spanish ever built in Canada.

Here's the church, where a stained-glass window commemorates the 1792 meeting between Captain George Vancouver and Captain Juan Francisco de la Bodega y Quadra. The meeting, overseen by the famed Chief Maquinna, was meant to resolve the dispute between Spain and Britain, which both claimed the site. Yuquot, once a key link in the international fur trade, was declared a national historic site in 1923.

Here's the lake with the tiny island that used to house the whalers' shrine, an ancient, sacred collection of ninety-two carved figures and sixteen human skulls, taken away by an anthropologist in 1905. The shrine has remained in storage in New York's American Museum of Natural History for a century.

Here's where the Mowachaht attacked the trading vessel *Boston* in 1803, killing twenty-five of its twenty-seven crewmen and lining their severed heads along the quarterdeck. It was the culmination of a series of violent incidents, including one in which the captain of the trading vessel *Sea Otter*, in retaliation for the theft of a chisel, opened fire with his cannon on the natives' canoes, slaughtering more than twenty men, women, and children.

The two survivors of the *Boston* massacre, including Jewitt, were taken as slaves by Maquinna. Jewitt—using quills from ravens and crows and writing in ink made by boiling blackberry juice with powdered charcoal, filtered through a cloth—kept a diary of his two years in captivity.

In 2003, the two-hundredth anniversary of the violent encounter, another John R. Jewitt, this one a Seattle math teacher and great-great-great-grandson of the captive, came to Yuquot as the guest of another Chief Maquinna, this one named Mike, as the Mowachaht/Muchalaht held their annual Summerfest celebration on Nootka Island.

Ray and Terry Williams enjoy Summerfest, enjoy the hikers and other visitors, too—but they also enjoy it when the stream of tourists dries up each fall, leaving them, and their ancestors, all alone for the winter, in their home of four thousand years.

the good deed that
went around the world

ONE DAY IN 2015, Victoria's Cedric Steele was in a business meeting when his assistant interrupted: "You have a call from Amsterdam—a Dr. Iain Reddish."

"Who's Iain Reddish?" wondered Steele. And so began one of the stranger, more uplifting pay-it-forward stories you'll ever hear.

The tale goes back to the end of 1968, when a twenty-four-year-old Steele, celebrating a hot start to what would become a long and successful real-estate career, treated himself to a holiday in the Bahamas.

Driving from the Nassau airport, Steele picked up a hitch-hiker. "He looked a little bit scraggly." A bit of a hippie, if you will.

The hitchhiker was British. He seemed to be an ambitious young man like Steele, but down on his luck.

Reddish remembered it like this: he was on a travelling scholarship but had lost his wallet. "I had no money what-soever. When I got out of the car, he said, 'You haven't any money, have you, kid?'"

Then Steele passed Reddish fifty US dollars. Reddish said he would repay him, but Steele held up his hand.

"I said, 'No need to pay me back,'" Steele later recalled. "I said, 'When you get established, if you find somebody you think needs a hand up, why don't you help them out and pass it on?'" Which is what Iain Reddish did, often, for the next forty-seven years.

He became an international environmental lobbyist, rattling political cages around the world. Everywhere he went—five continents, fifty or sixty countries—he picked up hitchhikers, sometimes buying them a coffee or a muffin, sometimes giving them a bit of money.

"Then I'd tell them the story of how Cedric stopped for me all those years ago." Pay it forward.

Almost half a century later, Reddish, then seventy, was at home in Amsterdam when he spied a bedraggled-looking man on the street. "He was standing outside my house, looking dishevelled."

"What are you doing here?" Reddish asked him.

"Trying to find work," replied the man, who had travelled to the Netherlands from Croatia.

Reddish took the man inside, fed him, gave him some money and—since they were the same build, standing six foot three—some clothes. ("He looked quite good in them," Reddish said.)

"You're a good man," the Croat said.

"I'm not the good man," Reddish replied. "Cedric Steele is the good man." And then Reddish started to relate his 1960s anecdote, telling the Croat of the guy who once gave him fifty dollars.

This is where things got seriously weird, in a good way.

"He interrupted me and said, 'I've heard this story before,'" Reddish said.

Pardon?

"He said, 'Aha, this happened in the Bahamas, didn't it?'"

Reddish was dumbfounded. It turns out the Croat had heard the story from a relative who had been travelling in

Africa. "His cousin was hitchhiking in Namibia last year and was picked up by someone who told him the story." Included in the Croat's account were a couple of details that confirmed it was the same tale.

Reddish had no idea how the story reached Namibia. He spent some time there in the 1990s doing work for Greenpeace International, but he couldn't recall giving anyone a lift. He was tickled to hear his own story echo back from the Croat, though.

So Reddish decided to look up Steele—whose name he had remembered all these years—to let him know he had become a global urban legend. Finding Steele in Victoria, where he had lived since 1975, took all of thirteen seconds on Google. Then Reddish made the phone call that was answered by Steele's assistant.

Steele, who is known in Victoria for his good citizenship, is glad Reddish made the effort.

"I had tears in my eyes," he says. "It's a heartwarming story."

Steele twice tried to meet Reddish in Europe after that, but Reddish was off on assignment for Greenpeace. They never did reconnect in person. Early in 2018, Steele learned Reddish had passed away—though his story continues its journey around the world.

cookies with hitler

RICHARD REITER USED to enjoy milk and cookies on the terrace of Adolf Hitler's house.

As a boy, he even called Hitler "Onkel Wolf"—Uncle Wolf—not as a term of endearment, but because Richard's aunt Mitzi was Hitler's girlfriend, and Wolf was her pet name for him. "I felt awkward around him. He felt awkward around us. He couldn't relate to children."

That was in the 1930s, in pre-war Berchtesgaden, where Richard and his brother would go to Hitler's Bavarian home and play with the Nazi leader's cherished Alsatian, Prinz.

"We loved playing with his dog. I guess that was the reason he let us in," said Reiter, sitting in the living room of his Oak Bay apartment in 2005. Hanging on the wall were three lithographs lifted from the German dictator's home after an air raid.

At age seventy-seven, Reiter had never told his story to the public before. A former soldier of the Waffen-SS and member of the Hitler Youth, he never hid his past, but didn't exactly shout about it either. He had good reason to remain circumspect—some readers were angry after Dave Obee and I told his tale in the *Times Colonist*, accusing us of glorifying a former Nazi. We didn't see it that way. We were just telling the fascinating story of an old man who had finally decided to talk.

Reiter was born in Berchtesgaden—"the Banff of Germany"—on April 22, 1928. That was two years after Hitler, then thirty-seven, met the sixteen-year-old Maria (Mitzi) Reiter, the woman some describe as the love of his life. Hitler was just the leader of the rising Nazi party at the time. She worked in the family-owned shop where he bought his Bavarian clothes. Hitler and Mitzi became romantically involved, much to the displeasure of Richard's father, Karl, who disapproved of his teenage sister's relationship with the older man. "My father gave him a tongue-lashing," Reiter said. Nevertheless, Hitler and Mitzi had an on-again, off-again relationship that lasted until 1938. He called her "Mimi."

From the age of five or six to the age of nine or ten, Richard met Hitler half a dozen times, mostly at Haus Wachenfeld, the house that Hitler began renting in 1924, then at the Berghof, the home he built on the same site in 1936. Richard and his brother, Günter, would have that milk and cookies and play with the dog.

It was telling that Hitler reserved his greatest affection for Prinz, Reiter said. "People who relate well to dogs have very poor people skills."

Certainly Hitler couldn't relate well to children, not in the easy, hugs-and-kidding manner of other adults. "He would stand and pat you on the head . . . It was very awkward."

Berchtesgaden, a town of a few thousand people, sits where the Bavarian Alps border Austria. It contains an area called Obersalzberg, which eventually became Nazi central, appropriated for the use of party leaders. Hitler had a house there. So did Reichsmarschall Hermann Goering.

"Albert Speer was a neighbour of ours," said Reiter. "Martin Bormann had the biggest house, because he had the most children."

Bormann and the party presented Hitler with another home, Kehlsteinhaus, the famed Eagle's Nest, high atop a mountain, as a fiftieth birthday present, but the dictator spent little time there, preferring the Berghof, which he had a hand in designing. (Obee and I learned about Reiter after the *Times Colonist* published a Hitler-drawn sketch of the Berghof but misidentified it as a hotel, leading Reiter to write the paper to correct the error.)

By the time war came, security was tight and the Nazi leaders' homes were off-limits to all. But such was not the case in the early 1930s, when Richard and Günter would visit Haus Wachenfeld.

"Meeting Hitler to us wasn't any big deal," Reiter said. "Hitler didn't become a myth until later."

More exciting were the rides in Hitler's big Mercedes, with his adjutant, Julius Schaup, at the wheel. Schaup once boarded with the Reiters and became a good family friend.

As Hitler's strength grew, Richard's father found himself in trouble. "My father was an outspoken socialist, so he was one of the first ones taken to Dachau." Karl was in and out of concentration camps from 1933 on, his politics landing him in custody, and Mitzi's intervention helping get him out.

Karl survived the war but was estranged from his family after his incarceration and his divorce from Richard's mother in 1938. "Because of our brainwashing, we began to reject him," Reiter said. Karl's alcohol abuse didn't help, either. Reiter did not see his father from 1938 until 1966. His father, by then a broken man, hanged himself shortly thereafter.

After his parents' divorce, the young Richard was shipped to Nazi-sponsored student residences in Budweis, Bohemia, and then, in January 1944, to the National Socialist Political Institution of Education in Munich—the school for the *crème de la crème* of Aryan youth.

"I was an ideal Nazi kid," Reiter said. "When I was fifteen years old, I was a colonel in the Hitler Youth already."

The school had its own 88-millimetre anti-aircraft battery, manned by the students, who would blast away at Allied bombers during air raids. "When the attack was over, we would run back to the classroom."

It was there that he learned what was going on at the concentration camps.

"I never denied the Holocaust, because I went to school with guys whose fathers were guards at Malthausen and Buchenwald," Reiter said. The students knew what the smokestacks meant. "It was whispered."

Later in life, Reiter would write to the Prime Minister, calling for Holocaust-denier Ernst Zündel's deportation from Canada. But in 1944, the young Richard was, like so many of his generation, still a true believer in his magnetic Fuhrer.

Hitler is often portrayed as a madman "biting the rug," Reiter said in 2005, but the truth is more chilling. This madman cut a compelling figure. "He had us totally captivated. When people compare [George W.] Bush to Hitler, I cringe, because Hitler could at least speak the language."

Hitler couldn't have timed his ascent better, feeding on the desperation and wounded pride of a nation left impoverished after the First World War, Reiter said. The Nazi was an opportunist who milked resentful German veterans' belief that it had been betrayal at home, not on the battlefront, that cost them the First World War. Germany's economic collapse was due to the harshness of another betrayal, the Treaty of Versailles, Hitler argued. "Half-truths served Hitler perfectly," Reiter said.

Hitler drew on desperation and nationalism, telling Germans their plight wasn't their fault, that it was deception at Versailles and the Jews who had brought them to grief. "There was Hitler saying, 'You were cheated. Follow me and I'll lead you to greatness again.' This is what people wanted to hear."

"There was a magic in Hitler, but it's the kind of magic you find in *Faust*, part 2, when he made a deal with the devil," Reiter said. "Look at Mitzi. She was a beautiful woman, but Hitler was a gnome. There had to be something."

That relationship gave the Reiter brothers an extra reason for being drawn to the Nazi leader. "We were so whipped up by Hitler's connection with Mitzi." (Mitzi ended up living with Hitler's sister, Paula, for a time after the war and later worked as a maid in a hotel. She died in the early 1990s in Hamburg, the home of her third husband, a badly wounded war veteran.)

In the fall of 1944, the brothers signed on with the Waffen-SS, the military wing that grew from the Nazi party's Schutzstaffel, or protective squadron. Sixteen-year-old Richard joined the First SS Panzer Division just in time to ride a Tiger tank into the Battle of the Bulge as a junker, or officer cadet. "We were full of piss and vinegar. We wanted to get in there."

The offensive, the only battle in which Richard took part, failed. "After two weeks we blew our own tanks up," Reiter said. "We had no more fuel."

The First SS Panzer Division, also known as the Adolf Hitler Division, was the Fuhrer's own guard. It contained two guard battalions, one of which was sent to protect Hitler in Berlin, the other—including Reiter—to the Nazi redoubt in southern Bavaria. On April 20—Hitler's birthday—with German resistance crumbling, the battalion set up base just south of Munich. It was also in that month that Günter was killed in action.

On April 25, in the last days of the war, Reiter was dispatched by motorcycle to Goering's house at Berchtesgaden to deliver an attaché case to the Waffen-SS battalion commander. No sooner had he delivered the pouch that morning than a nearby anti-aircraft battery opened fire. It was an air raid, British Lancaster bombers hammering Obersalzberg. "I ran to this one-man pillbox and locked myself inside." The pillbox was beside Goering's swimming pool, which took a direct hit. Reiter had to be dug out of the rubble.

The battalion commander fared worse. "The guy I gave the case to, he disintegrated." Reiter believed the attaché case contained Hitler's orders to execute Goering, whom the Nazi leader accused of treason. (Goering was arrested on Hitler's orders that day, but survived the war, only to take cyanide in 1946, the night before he was to hang for war crimes. Hitler himself committed suicide on April 30, 1945.)

Reiter made his way to the Berghof, which had been damaged in the raid. The lawn was littered with fire-damaged items tossed from the windows. Among them was a packing case containing works of art, many of them charred. He removed three pieces—lithographs of frescoes from the Sistine Chapel, copied for Hitler—that eventually found their way to Reiter's apartment wall in Oak Bay. "These were the only three that weren't scorched."

The next week, just two days before the end of the war, an American armoured personnel carrier shot the front off his motorcycle. "I crashed into the rocks." He cracked twelve vertebrae. Friends hid him in the mountains; no one wanted to be caught in an SS uniform.

After a few months, Reiter stopped hiding. He made his way to his mother's home in Berchtesgaden, staying there until four o'clock on the morning of St. Nicholas Day, December 6, 1945, when American troops burst in and arrested him at bayonet-point. They weren't gentle with SS men: "An older guy died that night because they beat him up."

Reiter was released in January 1946—with back pay from the Americans!—an early release he thinks was tied to an incident when he was in the Hitler Youth in Munich. When a Nazi official fired on captured Allied pilots, Richard hit him with his carbine. One of the pilots, a Lieutenant Cowing from Toronto, took Richard's name; he believed that record helped him in 1946.

Still, no one wanted to hire an SS veteran in 1946: "None of us could get jobs." Reiter turned to smuggling, carrying coffee and cigarettes from Austria, sometimes guiding people in the other direction.

One day he applied for work at an American recreation centre and was hired immediately because of his good command of English. He worked at the rec centre, managed an officers' club, and eventually began giving tours of Berchtesgaden for high-ranking Allied officials. Everyone wanted to go to Hitler's house. (In Oak Bay, Reiter still had photos of British generals and American judges from the I.G. Farben war crimes trial, as well as Alma Sonne, the president of the Mormon European Mission.)

Some of Reiter's well-connected friends tried to help him immigrate to the United States, but his Hitler Youth and Waffen-SS past prevented it. In 1948, he was suddenly ordered to appear before a denazification court. Even though he had served as a soldier in the Waffen-SS, not as a black-shirt in the notorious political wing, his membership in the SS, deemed a criminal organization, earned him a sentence of three years hard labour.

Reiter served two weeks. While road-building in the mountains, he strapped on his skis and took off for Austria, where an American friend got him false papers. In Austria, he worked for the US Army's Information Services Branch. (His identity card from those days bore a "denazification" stamp dated 1950.) One day, in Salzburg, he saw a sign advertising immigration to Canada. When he looked into the idea, no one asked about the Hitler Youth or SS. As an old man, Reiter still had his assisted-passage agreement, in which he promised to repay the Canadian government for his fare on the SS *Italia*.

On Reiter's first day in Toronto, he got a job working the desk at the Royal York and checked actor Jimmy Durante into the hotel. Eventually he married a Canadian girl, had a family, and became a teacher, working in New Brunswick, Quebec, and Toronto. He didn't volunteer much about his past, but said he answered honestly if asked. When offered a job at Toronto's Forest Hills Junior High, where he taught history and geography from 1960 to 1978, he told the principal that he had been in the Hitler Youth and SS.

After his wife died, Reiter married his childhood sweetheart and moved back to Austria for fifteen years. Following the death of his second wife, he moved to Oak Bay in 2003.

Reiter's own redemption took time, his views changing over the years as he read history, looking for the truth. "It was very gradual. I couldn't put a date on it."

But it was in Austria that he realized how much his views had changed. He couldn't stomach the popular attitude, which held that a "little Hitler" would be good for the country.

"People would say, 'Hitler was a bad guy, but . . . '" It was the *but* that bothered him.

He also heard echoes of Nazi Germany in the United States, where a mixture of fear, anger, nationalism, and a sense of superiority and entitlement were driving the agenda. Witness the Pax Americana enforced on Iraq and elsewhere. Manifest destiny, rekindled.

The difference, Reiter said, is that in Germany the Nazis used a propaganda machine to push their message from the top down. "In the United States, it's a grassroots movement that's coming from the bottom up."

What about Canada? Could a Hitler, a Nazi party, ever succeed here?

"Never," he replied, emphatically.

Richard Reiter died in Ontario in 2017.

skating across canada

ONE DAY IN 1966, Clint Shaw had just come home from his job at Canada Packers in Vancouver and was eating his supper while watching TV, when a commercial came on showing a guy playing a tuba on top of a mountain.

The tuba played the first four notes of "O Canada." Then a tickertape message ran across the screen: "What are you, as a proud Canadian, going to do to celebrate Centennial year?"

Good question, thought Shaw.

That's how he came to roller skate across Canada, in an odyssey that began in Victoria in April 1967. The 7,900-kilometre effort landed him in the Guinness World Records book. He earned another entry in 1974 when he became the first person to skate across the United States. He earned two other records, too.

But let's not get ahead of ourselves.

Clint Shaw wanted to mark Canada's Centennial by crossing the country in a manner that hadn't been done before. He settled on roller skating, which he hadn't done since age five.

His wife, the mother of their two preschool-age daughters, wasn't thrilled. Good luck, she said, but don't expect us to be here when you get back.

So Shaw, then twenty-five, had just a few friends and relations around when he set out from Mile Zero, the westernmost point of the Trans-Canada Highway. "I dunked my skates in the ocean at Dallas and Douglas, then I got on the road and started skating for St. John's, Newfoundland."

By the time he got to the Lower Mainland, his wife had relented. She piled the kids into their four-door Ford Fairlane 500 and followed him to Hope, which is where he ended up in hospital after his left leg went numb.

No more skating for you, the doctor said, but Shaw gave it just a month before picking up where he left off, this time with the family in a truck and camper.

It was hard going, day after day of skating toward traffic— no helmet, no pads—night after night of bunking in the camper. Some moments have stayed with him. "When you have people brush by you doing one hundred miles per hour, that sticks out."

Shaw desperately wanted a sponsor, but sponsors desperately didn't want him, so he ended up relying on his parents.

He was also wearing crappy skates. A Canadian Press story of the day noted he had gone through forty-four wheels, five axles, and so many ball bearings he had lost count by the time he reached Regina. ("Roller Skater Loses Bearings," read the headline in the Victoria *Daily Colonist*.)

Regina is where Shaw met former prime minister John Diefenbaker. The sitting prime minister, Lester Pearson, greeted him in Ottawa. All the Shaws were treated like royalty at Expo 67 in Montreal, ushered to the front of every line. Newfoundland's flamboyant premier, Joey Smallwood, was waiting when Shaw finally rolled into St. John's.

That wasn't until 1968, though. By November 11, 1967, the Shaws had made it as far as Rivière-du-Loup, Quebec, before packing it in for the winter. Shaw resumed his journey the next August 29—his birthday—this time going solo until reaching Newfoundland that fall.

You would think that would be enough skating for one life, right?

Wrong.

"Seven years later, I found out nobody had done the States."

By then Shaw was living in Victoria, employed as an ironworker. The 1974 US trip was much smoother than the Centennial slog. Shaw had decent skates. He had a sponsor in Pepsi. ("Join the Pepsi People . . . feelin' free!" read his T-shirt.) The soft drink company would hand over five hundred dollars every time he hit a certain landmark. "It was like playing Monopoly and passing Go."

The US media loved him. *Time* magazine, gushing about his physique, said he resembled Clint Eastwood. Shaw appeared on *The Tomorrow Show, Hollywood Squares*, and *The Joey Bishop Show*. Newspapers lined up.

"He sounded crazy and he was," wrote the *Record-Herald* of Washington Court House (yes, that's the name of a city), Ohio. "He had a wild look in his eyes—the kind of look only a man overflowing with life can have—and he was. He looked at you when he told of his adventures and you felt his surplus energy rushing over you and you wanted to go with him."

It took just sixty-two days to skate the five thousand kilometres from New York to Los Angeles, which brought his second Guinness mention. A third record was set en route when he broke one hundred miles one scorching-then-freezing day in New Mexico.

By then he had a taste for Guinness (the printed version). In 1975 he headed to Reseda, California, to set a roller-skating marathon record: seven days, fifteen hours, and seven minutes. A young Connie Chung skated with him during that effort. So did Three Dog Night drummer Floyd Sneed, Shaw's childhood friend from Calgary.

After the Reseda marathon was done, a photographer snapped Shaw's picture. "Then I took my skates off and I never put them on again."

Those skates live in the BC Sports Hall of Fame in BC Place now. Shaw lives in Campbell River.

In 2017, he hit the road again. "I'm redoing the trip," he said, on the phone from Calgary. Started in Beacon Hill Park, heading for St. John's.

Skating?

Hell no.

"I'm driving across. At seventy-five, I'm not about to put on my skates."

So why do it in 1967?

"Because it was Centennial year and I'm a proud Canadian."

alban michael

———

ONE NIGHT WHEN seventy-eight-year-old Alban Michael was in hospital with pneumonia, his parents came to him in a dream. They spoke Nuchatlaht, just like when he was a boy on Nootka Island.

Alban's dreams were, in fact, the only place such a conversation could take place. Of the seven billion people on Earth, the Vancouver Island man was the very last one fluent in his mother tongue.

"I'm the only one now," he said, slowly. It made him sad.

And now he's gone. Alban Michael died in 2016 at age eighty-nine.

When I wrote about Alban a decade earlier, it was as the personification of the fragility of the Island's rapidly vanishing native languages. Like stars blinking out in the sky, the people who still spoke the likes of SENĆOŦEN, Lekwungen, and Hul'q'umi'num' were quietly, rapidly disappearing.

That's still the case today. There's a race against time to record, even revive, traditional languages. Some dismiss that as a pointless pursuit of the arcane, but to others it's the key to retaining identity—no language, no culture. Lose a language and you draw the blinds on a window offering a different view of the world.

On the day I met Alban, he sat sipping tea in his tidy little house on the tiny Nuchatlaht reserve at Oclucje—pronounced "OO-cloo-gee"—twelve kilometres down a perilous logging road from Zeballos, way up on northern Vancouver Island.

At his doorstep was the head of Espinosa Inlet, where just a few days before, he and wife Rose had been treated to the spectacle of sea lions and killer whales fighting just off shore. ("They were jumping up above the water," said Rose. "I had never seen that before. Wow, what a good movie.") The Michaels had a smokehouse out back, ate plenty of cod, halibut, salmon—*suuha*, the Nuu-chah-nulth people call the latter.

Raised at Nuchatlitz on Nootka Island, Alban didn't learn English until he landed at residential school in Tofino. An English-only rule was enforced at such institutions, sometimes with a strap.

"We weren't supposed to talk native, eh?" said Alban. Call it cultural genocide, or call it a well-meaning belief of paternalistic authorities that Indigenous people would have to assimilate to survive, the effect was the same: whole generations of Indigenous people lost their first languages.

It was only because of his unilingual mother that Alban kept his Nuchatlaht. "That's how I held on to the language. I used to talk to my mother. I couldn't speak English to her."

It came in handy later when he was gill netting salmon in Nootka Sound and didn't want strangers listening when he radioed another boat. "When I wanted to keep a secret, I spoke my language."

Rose spoke an entirely different language, Kwak'wala, so English became the common tongue at home. When Alban's father died in the 1990s, so did Alban's last chance to converse in Nuchatlaht.

NUCHATLAHT IS A branch of Nuu-chah-nulth, some of whose dialects are so diverse that many consider them separate, and therefore more fragile, languages. For example, Alban could speak with a friend from the nearby Mowachaht band whose dialect was close enough to be understood. "And I understand them in Ahousaht," he added. But that was about it.

By 2018 just 134 members of fourteen Nuu-chah-nulth communities scattered down the west coast of Vancouver Island were fluent in any of the dialects, according to the Brentwood Bay–based First Peoples' Cultural Council, a BC Crown corporation that has been leading language-revitalization efforts.

Nuu-chah-nulth belongs to the Wakashan family of languages. Other Wakashan languages on Vancouver Island are Ditidaht (spoken by seven people around Nitinat Lake) and Kwak'wala. In 2018 a total of 165 people were still fluent in the five dialects of the latter, the language of the Kwakwaka'wakw, who inhabit the inner coast and islands from Campbell River north.

Languages of a second family, Salishan, are found from Sooke to Victoria and all the way up to the Comox Valley. In 2018, just seven people were fully comfortable in any of the five related Straits Salish dialects—T'Sou-ke, Malchosen, Lekwungen, SENĆOŦEN, and Semiahmoo—traced from Sooke to the tip of the Saanich Peninsula and over to Tsawwassen and Surrey. (Klallam, which was spoken at Becher Bay, by Metchosin, is a separate language.) Farther north, Hul'q'umi'num'—found, with some dialect differences, from Cowichan Bay to Nanoose—is one of three related Coast Salish dialects (the other two are on the Lower Mainland) that were still spoken by ninety-three people. Another forty-seven people, spanning the strait from the Comox Valley to the mainland, spoke the language of the K'ómoks-Sliammon. But Pentlatch, heard in the Courtenay area, faded away in the first half of the twentieth century.

Some languages are fairly close to one another, in the manner of Norwegian and Swedish, making it relatively easy for someone from Sooke to talk to someone from Saanich.

Other linguistic gaps are wider. A Hul'q'umi'num' speaker from Duncan could, with effort, talk to a SENĆOŦEN speaker from the Saanich Peninsula in the same way that people from the north of England could once make out the language of Dutch Friesians. "They're far enough apart that it's not a walk in the park," said University of Victoria linguist Tom Hukari.

Those Salishan speakers would not have a hope of understanding a Wakashan language, though. Cross the hump from Port Alberni to Parksville and you'll find languages "as distinct as Russian is from Congolese," said historian Ron Hamilton, a Hupačasath man from the Alberni area.

"We live thirty miles apart but speak 100 percent different languages."

Speak, that is, if you can still find people who know the languages.

WHEN DUNCAN'S ABNER THORNE wanted a real Hul'q'umi'num' gab-fest, he had to seek out octogenarian chums like Angus Smith or Ross Modeste. "That's about the only time I use it now," he said in 2005.

Too bad, the then-seventy-eight-year-old added, because there are some Hul'q'umi'num' words that just won't translate. Try to convey the same thing in English and you've got to take the long way around.

When Thorne was a boy in the 1930s, all the Cowichan people spoke their own language. Some even had trouble pronouncing his first name, Abner. Epnah, they called him, there being no "b" or "r" sound in Hul'q'umi'num'. (Nor does it have an "f" or "v." The name *Violet* is pronounced "Piolet." *Victoria* becomes "Matulia.")

"It was the only language I heard when I was growing up," Thorne said.

He didn't learn English until he walked to Koksilah Indian Day School. "At school, you had to speak English. We were careful not to speak Hul'q'umi'num'. You got strapped, eh? Or made to stand in the corner."

That Thorne remained as fluent in Hul'q'umi'num' as in English reflected the fact that he had Hul'q'umi'num'-speaking family and neighbours around, unlike the kids isolated in residential schools.

He figured he was fully comfortable with English by age fourteen or fifteen. In 1942, at sixteen, he bought one of the gillnetters the government had seized from fishermen of Japanese descent during the Second World War. Commercial fishing had its own lexicon. "We used English most of the time." It was probably in the 1950s, he said, that English became the dominant language of the Cowichan.

Efforts are now being made to teach Hul'q'umi'num' to the young, but it's a different sound that emerges when they speak.

"The dialect is changing, influenced by the English tongue," Thorne said. Disappearing is the distinctive accent associated with Indigenous people. Kids today speak with a hard English "k," not the thick, back-of-the-tongue sound of their grandparents, and have trouble wrapping their mouths around the old sounds.

"Some of our people interject English into their Hul'q'umi'num' words."

Languages can adapt to change. Hul'q'umi'num', which once only had words for the seasons, grew to include words for the months and days of the week, said Thorne. He couldn't tell you the word for computer, but car is *sun'un'hwul*—literally, canoe.

Hul'q'umi'num' also has words for harrow, plow, and other farm implements that arrived with the Europeans, proving languages can adapt to changing times. It's a matter of making the effort.

BUT WHY MAKE that effort? Does it really matter if a language goes extinct? Yes, said Hamilton: "It provides another tool for thinking about and solving problems." Think of the biodiversity principle, which argues for the preservation of species if only because we don't yet know their true value.

Up in Alert Bay, Andrea Sanborn—then the executive director of the U'mista Cultural Centre, where they held twice-a-week classes in Kwak'wala—was blunt about what retention means: "Without our language, we aren't Kwakwaka'wakw."

That thought—or, rather, the idea that the language would disappear—is what haunted Pauline Alfred, too. Beginning in 1976, she taught Kwak'wala at Alert Bay's First Nations school for close to a quarter century. Alfred's fluency was due in part to geography. Across the strait on Kingcome Inlet, where she was born in 1939, frozen waters in parts of the inlet created cultural barriers behind which Indigenous people could keep the old ways alive.

"We danced and danced all winter. They didn't know we were dancing up there," she recalled in 2002. "We kept our culture really strong."

And then came the day when, at age six, she was taken away to the Anglican-run residential school in Alert Bay. "I didn't know a word of English. My first language was Kwak'wala."

For the next seven years, she endured the now-familiar story: "Wham, we got slapped, or had our hair pulled, if they heard us speaking Kwak'wala. How did they expect us to talk?"

The residential schools erased native languages for many. But summers back home at Kingcome, or on Gilford Island, made the difference for Alfred. "When we went home, all we heard was Kwak'wala." She called it a beautifully nuanced language, laced with such terms of endearment as k'wala'yu, which means "you're my reason for living." Try that one on your wife, she suggested. (I did. My wife replied with an eye-rolling "Whatever.")

Alfred said you would bust a gut if she told you a joke in Kwak'wala. "My language is a very descriptive language. It's a thousand times funnier than English. You'll laugh for an hour."

By the arrival of the new millennium, Kwak'wala was still what flowed naturally when Alfred was on the phone to her siblings. "I am a big-time survivor of the residential school system," she said proudly. "I can still speak my native tongue."

She credited her grandmother and her grandmother's brothers and sisters with passing on the old ways, which Alfred called upon when overseeing potlatches, held when there were weddings, or memorials, when a chieftainship is passed, or when kids were given names and rights in the Big House.

Language, she said, was woven into everything: traditional foods, history, land, treasure boxes. Every Kwakwaka'wakw family owns a treasure box, she explained. It is a set of rights to things both tangible and intangible: songs, masks, dances, blankets, names.

IF SOME OF the concepts were a little difficult to grasp for White Boy here (as was the pronunciation of *Kwakwaka'wakw*; try "KWOK-kwok-ya-wokw") it was quickly evident that there was a complex and deeply rooted way of life that infused, to varying degrees, everyday existence among the Indigenous people of Alert Bay. It was evident in everything from diet to the definition of family.

This was important, because just as being Scottish involves more than throwing on a kilt on Robbie Burns Day, sustaining Indigenous culture means living the traditions. Examples abound. The skeleton of the first salmon of the year gets tossed into the ocean as a sign of gratitude. When there's a food fishery, the chiefs and elders are taken care of first. The fish might end up getting bartered for herring roe or elk meat.

Each spring, fishermen from Alert Bay cross over to Knight Inlet to net eulachon, members of the smelt family prized for their oil. The fish are ripened for several days in pits dug on the riverbank, then cooked in freshwater, with the oil skimmed off the surface and repeatedly screened to remove impurities before being bottled. By the time the boats get back to Alert Bay with the haul—a thousand litres in a good year, though there are fewer of those these days—the oil has set into a buttery paste. ("I sure would like to taste that," I once hinted to one of the men carefully unloading the jugs from a seiner. "I bet you would," he replied, and kept on unloading.)

At least once a week, Alfred would make a fish soup flavoured with eulachon grease and sprinkled with seaweed. "Man, that's good when you've got a cold," she said.

All of which illustrates that Alfred isn't just some cobwebbed academic muttering wistfully about a dead language. She is a woman concerned for a living culture.

"I see the emergency light flashing off and on now," she said. "People have to get very serious and get in there to preserve our language. It's the root of our identity."

That's why, when she taught Kwak'wala, it bothered her that the language rarely made it out of the classroom.

"Look at those kids," she said, pointing to the children of the owners of Alert Bay's Chinese restaurant one day in 2002. "They speak Chinese to their parents. Why don't our youth speak Kwak'wala?"

The truth is, it will be hard for either Kwak'wala or Chinese to survive on Vancouver Island. Look at the typical immigrant family: without a geographic and population base to cling to, it's hard for any minority language to tread water for more than a generation or two before going under. Chances are, if your grandparents came to BC speaking something other than English, you can't speak their mother tongue. Language champions are fighting the tide.

THAT LANGUAGES DIE is not new, but the pace of change is increasing in the electronic age. Around the globe, local cultures are being rapidly overwhelmed by Hollywood, YouTube, and whatever else comes through the headphones or over your iPhone.

In his book *Spoken Here: Travels among Threatened Languages*, Canadian author Mark Abley cited estimates that up to half of the six thousand languages still spoken in the world today will disappear within a couple of generations. That's important not just to those within the associated cultures, but to all of us. "What the survival of threatened languages means, perhaps, is the endurance of dozens, hundreds, thousands of subtly different notions of truth," he argues.

The thing is—and this is critically important—"threatened" doesn't mean "dead." Vancouver Island's Indigenous languages might be on life support, but they are still alive—and, in some cases, showing signs of regaining their health.

This is the story that language champions want heard—and a reason why some squirm at last-speaker tales like Alban's, which they worry send the message that Indigenous languages are a lost cause, not worth the fight to preserve.

In truth, vigorous efforts are being made to not only record and preserve but revitalize languages. The efforts come in a variety of forms. Four bands collaborated on a phrase book and dictionary of the Barkley Sound dialect of Nuu-chah-nulth in 2004. A dictionary of SENĆOŦEN, the language of the Saanich Peninsula, was expected in the summer of 2018. At the same time, directional signs recently erected in downtown Victoria display both Lekwungen and English geographic names. Bus information has been printed in SENĆOŦEN, for BC Transit passengers in Victoria, and in Hul'q'umi'num' for those in Nanaimo. In 2015, when Port Hardy's Joye Walkus graduated from the University of Victoria, a centuries-old Chilkat blanket draped around her shoulders, she was part of the very first cohort to earn a bachelor of education in Indigenous language revitalization. That means she can teach the whole K–12 curriculum in Kwak'wala.

Some of the most intensive efforts are being made through the First Peoples' Cultural Council, working from offices at the Tsartlip First Nation in Brentwood Bay. Its FirstVoices project offers an Internet-based digital archive to which people can contribute and draw upon text and audio and video recordings. By 2016, FirstVoices had documented portions of twenty-three of BC's thirty-four Indigenous languages and thirty-eight of ninety-five dialects, though none had been recorded completely. (Alban Michael's voice can be heard speaking some of the 1,125 words and 1,215 phrases archived in the part of the database dedicated to the Nuchatlaht and Ehattesaht dialects.)

A recent breakthrough was the development of downloadable Indigenous-language fonts. That helped address one linguistic hurdle: The lack of a traditional Indigenous orthography, or system of spelling. Some sounds can't be replicated on a standard keyboard. Trying to do so is like rowing a boat with a fork.

Nuu-chah-nulth, for example, doesn't have "b," "d," "f," "g," "j," "l," "r," "v," or "z" sounds, though it does have fourteen sounds not found in English. Other Indigenous languages have a whole range of "g" and "k" sounds that English speakers find hard to imitate. The subtleties can fool non-Indigenous ears; in Campbell River, for example, you'll find the same word spelled variously as Yucalta, Euclataws, Ligwilda'xw, and Laich-wil-tach.

"There are some sounds that English just doesn't have," says John Elliott, one of the driving forces behind the revitalization of SENĆOŦEN, which includes four "k" sounds (eight if you include the *c*'s and *q*'s).

To compensate, linguists sprinkle a variety of symbols— hyphens, apostrophes, even numerals—through Indigenous words to represent sounds not found in English. A straight apostrophe, for example, can denote a glottal stop—a slight pause in a word, like the silence that replaces the missing consonants when Cockneys drop the *t*'s in the word *bottle*. The straight apostrophe can also denote a glottalized sound, one with a bit of "pop" to it.

Some written versions have symbols not found on keyboards at all. The Nuu-chah-nulth dictionary includes one character resembling a backwards question mark, another that looks like a letter *k* that's been smacked with a flyswatter.

There are other encouraging signs: while fluent speakers are fading away, the opposite is true of those who are considered semi-fluent. By 2014 their number had shot up to more than 12,000 from 3,144 in 2010. Close to a third of them were under age twenty-five. Almost one in ten Indigenous people are actively learning their languages, whether as children or adults, says the Cultural Council. They got a major boost in 2018 when the provincial government announced it was setting aside $50 million for language revitalization, to be administered by the council.

ONE OF THE most promising signs is at the ȽÁU, WELNEW Tribal School, a couple of kilometres away from the Cultural Council offices. Run by the W̱SÁNEĆ School Board, it has included a SENĆOŦEN immersion program since 2013. The kids who were in Kindergarten then were in Grade 4 by the spring of 2018, by which time enrolment had grown to ninety students. The program will continue to expand as that lead cohort ages—Grade 5, then Grade 6, and so on—and as the University of Victoria certifies more SENĆOŦEN-speaking teachers. There are nine of the latter now, all of them running with the torch passed down by John Elliott and others of his generation. It's pretty much like French Immersion, the teachers perhaps not fully fluent in the language of instruction but proficient enough to teach it (and the children speaking one language inside the classroom but English, or a mixture, outside).

I ducked in for a look one day in May, arriving just in time to see the day's designated leader, a smiling, ponytailed seven-year-old girl in a mauve T-shirt, greet her schoolmates, ask them about the weather, and throw in a couple of other questions—all in SENĆOŦEN—to which they reply in unison. Then they all danced and sang a song about the thirteen-moon calendar's current month, PEXSISEN, the "moon of the opening hand," meaning the time when things blossom. Following that was a song about the SX̱ÁNEȽ—bullheads— that hide under rocks to lay eggs and that make a squeaking sound as the old-timers pry them out—a springtime delicacy— with sticks.

A few minutes later, in the Grade 4 classroom, a girl perched on a stool, swinging her pink-sandalled feet during a SENĆOŦEN version of show-and-tell. She delivered 90 percent of it in that language, pausing only to ask teacher Jim Elliott for help translating a few words ("bubbles, you know, those big ones") while dropping in the odd reference to Reese's Pieces and Oh Henry! bars (apparently her news was chocolate-based).

Just down the hall, Elisha Elliott was teaching her Grade 2s how to tell time on a clock. Seven o'clock was relatively easy, sounding like "tsoqus teentun," but 7:15 was more challenging, sounding (sort of) like "tsoqus ee opun eeuks lkachus," with the *l* in that last word made by placing the tip of the tongue at the top of the mouth and breathing through that, and the subsequent *k* coming from way back in the throat.

"Oh my God, that's a lot," blurted out one boy. Yes, it is— but it's also pretty cool to see children speaking an Indigenous language. When was the last time you heard that?

That's why, as the school day begins, the teachers make a point of walking the children past the building housing the adult learning centre. It's to show the elders who work there that all those years of trying to keep the language going have paid off.

On this morning, elder Lou Claxton was slumped in a chair, ear buds plugged into a computer, Skyping with a linguist at the University of Northern Texas. Claxton is one of only three remaining people—another is in Nanaimo, the third in Becher Bay—to speak SENĆOŦEN as their first language. Pulling vocabulary out of his memory is like panning for gold.

Across the room, John Elliott, Belinda Claxton, and Ian Sam were talking about that soon-to-be published dictionary. Fifteen years ago, Belinda wouldn't have believed SENĆOŦEN would be spoken at all, let alone be growing. "We thought it was gone."

The turning point came when the University of Victoria funded a revitalization program. "That's what saved us," she said. Those revitalization efforts now sit on a solid foundation: a written version of the language, a dictionary, a school in which to learn, an immersion program, teachers.

Now things are at the point where Sam, who has three children in the immersion program, can converse with them in everyday life. "At my house, I speak SENĆOŦEN to them all the time."

That's a great picture, but it's also a relative rarity, an exception that demonstrates how much remains to be done. "I would say this language is still critically endangered," Elliott said. "When we have the language being spoken at the dinner table and the breakfast table, then we'll be there."

AS IT IS, the people who grew up speaking that way—the ones who, like Alban Michael, actually dream in the old languages—

are fading away. Alban, his wife, Rose, and Abner Thorne are all gone now.

Back in 2005, Rose, looking out the window of her house in the Nuchatlaht community, watched her husband slowly pick his way toward the beach.

"It sounds really nice when you hear him talking," she said.

Yes, it did.

defender of the deer

THE KNOCK ON those who oppose culling urban deer is that they themselves are urban animals—latte-sucking city dwellers with a Disneyfied view of nature. Which, for the anti-cull crowd's most familiar face, is as far from reality as the isolated lighthouses in which she was raised.

Kelly Carson, the founder of DeerSafe Victoria, grew up surrounded by animals, not people. That shaped who she is.

Born in Vancouver, she was six years old when she moved to McInnes Island, forty kilometres west of Bella Bella, with her younger brother, mother, and lighthouse-keeper stepfather.

"I remember the day we landed," she says. "There was a blizzard . . . We had to jump onto the rocks." They weren't dressed for the weather, so the fellow driving the boat gave each of the kids one of his mittens.

From the ravens who stole her toys to the mink in the garden, animals were her only companions. But no, it wasn't Disney. She remembers sea lions scrambling onto the rocks to escape the orcas. One fell off. "The water turned red."

Once, while peering into a tidal pool, she gave little thought to a pod of whales in the distance—until one shot over to check her out, suddenly looming up so close that its dorsal fin filled her vision before it silently sank away. "It didn't occur to me until years later that I could have been lunch."

When she was eight, another sea lion pulled onto the rocks, pursued by a commercial fishboat. A fisherman, brandishing a rifle, motioned to her to move out of the way of his shot. She refused. "I just stood there. I wasn't going to leave."

She was still eight when the family moved to Egg Island, fifty-five kilometres north of Port Hardy. It was her home for eleven years. Another family shared lightkeeping duties, but that was it for human contact. "There were never any kids our age." Her hands would shake with nerves when helicopters or boat crews—strangers—would land on the island. "Life on the lights in the 1960s and '80s was beautiful, and not something I would wish on anyone," she now says.

The family's one-month annual leave was usually spent in Vancouver, but for a three-year stretch in her mid-teens, Carson didn't see civilization at all. Instead, vacations were spent boating around the coast. It was at Bella Bella that she first saw "casual violence" against animals, kids having "drowning races" to get rid of unwanted kittens and puppies as directed by their parents. With no vet to spay and neuter pets and keep the dog population under control, the Mounties would periodically shoot those deemed to have turned feral.

When Carson finally hit the city, moving to Vancouver at age nineteen, it was culture shock. She couldn't get used to being in a car, had never owned a television (still doesn't), didn't know what people were talking about much of the time. "I would talk about animals and birds, because that's what I knew, but people's eyes would glaze over, so I stopped talking about that."

Carson was still nineteen when she had her first child, the second arriving a couple of years later. She persuaded her husband to be a lightkeeper ("I said there would be no Hydro bills and no rent") and headed for the station at Pachena Point on the west coast of Vancouver Island, then to another at Cape Scott on its northern tip. Lots of mammals this time: bears, wolves, cougars. And deer, of course. When they wiped out her garden at Cape Scott, it meant no fresh vegetables for a family whose only other source of food was a supply ship.

In the mid-1980s, when her eldest reached school age, the family moved to Victoria. Carson, who works for the government, has been there ever since.

After the University of Victoria decided to cull the hundreds of rabbits living wild on campus, Carson was part of a group that relocated more than six hundred of the bunnies to Coombs in 2010. "That experience taught me that we're not helpless. It taught me that if you organize, you can make a difference."

When the killing of urban deer came up for debate around Victoria in 2012, she founded DeerSafe. Advocating for the deer was not always a pleasant experience. Even animal lovers aren't always sold on her cause, as she found while gathering signatures on a petition against a deer cull in Oak Bay. "I'll be standing on a corner and people will come within inches of my face and scream at me." She doesn't enjoy that. Nor does she like speaking to crowds or using a bullhorn.

Still, she forges on. She's the president of the BC Deer Protection Society and writes regularly for the *Victoria Animal News* on topics from a 2017 plan to cull deer in a Salt Spring Island nature preserve to a 2018 hunter-driven campaign to trap and kill wolves in BC. That last one resulted in an envelope with no return address being mailed to her home. Inside was a photo of three hanging wolves. Scrawled on the back in a childish hand was a note telling her to expect more and to keep up the good work. Nice.

"This is getting to be like housework," she says. "It never ends."

Carson—a vegan for a dozen years, vegetarian for more than twice that—keeps at it because she feels compelled to stand up for her beliefs.

"I'm just trying to do no harm."

addiction

OF ALL THE people sucked into the vortex of drug addiction, Ken Robinson was among the last you would expect to die violently.

He was a likable guy, a cheerful, chatty pepperpot, if a bit on the thin and grizzled side. He died in Victoria in 2005 at age fifty-three, stabbed to death in the entrance to a Wark Street apartment building.

Drug dealer James Kennedy, to whom Robinson owed money, later pleaded guilty to murder and was sentenced to life with no parole for ten years. Kennedy's girlfriend got two years for her role. Another man, whose role was limited to using his truck to cut off Robinson as he bicycled down the street, received probation.

It would be easy to dismiss this as just another drug murder. That's pretty much what I did until learning the identity of the victim.

Robinson was a barber—my barber, for a while. It was a trade he learned in prison, where he served time for, in his words, "being young and stupid" back in the early 1970s. He once told me he had got mixed up with some bad guys, and one night found himself bound to a chair and gun-whipped by some other bad guys in a drug rip-off in the Helmcken Road area of Saanich. Police nabbed the lot of them and Robinson wound up inside, learning to cut hair.

One day, the man who had attacked Robinson was marched into the prison, and later into Robinson's barber chair, where the inmate sat trembling like a leaf as Robinson stood over him with a straight razor. "Don't worry," said Robinson. "I won't hurt you."

It's hard to imagine Ken Robinson hurting anyone. Police, clients, and colleagues all described him as not having a mean bone in his body. He was friendly and loquacious whenever I spoke with him, at one point talking eagerly about getting his old rock 'n' roll band back together. He seemed proud of having put his past behind him.

Apparently it's not that easy. Addiction isn't discriminating, won't ease its grip just because you're a good person who made some bad choices.

Robinson's bad choices were made young. The boy who loved soccer and music ended up addicted to heroin. "Ken is an actual victim of marijuana as a gateway drug," his father, Dave, says. Robinson fell in with a notorious Victoria crowd that included the likes of Jimmy Page and Joseph Pagnotta, both now dead. Pagnotta's own struggle with addiction ended in February 2004 when the knife-wielding man was shot dead by RCMP outside his Langford home.

Robinson went straight in the mid-1970s. He stayed clean for eighteen years, opened his own barber shop on Quadra Street. It was decked out in black and gold, the colours of his favourite team, the Pittsburgh Steelers.

Then, in 1995, drugs re-entered his life. One of his old buddies showed up and dangled the dope in front of him, his father said.

Robinson kept struggling back. He moved in with his parents for a few years, worked at another barber shop, was doing pretty well until two or three years before his death. That's when the last decline began.

"As parents, we were so bloody helpless," Dave says. Robinson stopped working. He was beaten up a couple of times in the year before his murder, something from which he tried to shield his parents.

"He kept this very, very secret and he did everything in his power to make sure we weren't involved in it," Dave says, just a couple of days after losing his son. Robinson had last visited his parents a couple of weeks earlier.

Dave worked at the Wilkinson Road jail for fifteen years and knows what addiction can drive people to do. He appreciates how Robinson didn't allow desperation to get the best of him.

"He was honest with everybody," Dave says. "I am one parent who had a son addicted to drugs who never stole from him. He never took a thing from the house, never took any money."

Robinson's parents learned a lot about addiction over thirty-five years, learned how to distinguish between their son and the disease that held him.

"We never had anything but respect for him," his dad says. "We love him dearly."

the revolving door

ALLAN FRECHETTE COULD tell you exactly when he quit using drugs. It was July 25, 1995, the night he stabbed Kenneth Harris to death in Victoria's Blanshard Court while stoned on cocaine and magic mushrooms.

Up until then, Frechette's story was merely depressingly familiar. Abusive upbringing in Port Alberni, into drugs and crime by twenty, a revolving door in and out of prison by twenty-one.

When inside, he just became harder, meaner, more bitter. When they let him out, he broke into your house. He figured he pulled five hundred to one thousand break-ins through the late 1980s and early '90s, up and down Vancouver Island, around the Lower Mainland. He did it to fuel a $400-a-day cocaine habit and an addiction to the rush he got from crime.

So the question he pondered when I interviewed him in September 2000, sitting in a windowless little room in Wilkinson Road jail, is how you prevent guys from becoming another Allan Frechette. How do you break someone out of that all-too-predictable spiral that always seems to lead back to prison and has the rest of us cursing as we tally the physical and emotional cost of burglary, of violence, of living in a society in which everything must be kept under lock and key?

Frechette answered confidently but politely, his gaze unwavering—at thirty-three years of age he had the voice of experience. Already behind bars for five years, he had just lost a retrial of his murder case and was preparing to ship out to a federal prison.

Property crime is driven by the need to pay for drugs, he began. It's impossible to stop the flow of narcotics, so to stop users from using, you have to pick them off, one by one, when they're in prison and ripe for a change.

You have to catch them young, before they're immersed in the life, before their heads are too twisted.

You have to keep the kids apart from the older inmates who will abuse, school, and harden them until the kids are as hard as their abusers.

And, he stressed, you have to give them a replacement for their addiction, an alternative just as thrilling as the drugs and crime you want them to drop.

"You have to catch each person individually and give them that alternative and give them something to live for."

Maybe that's an Outward Bound course, maybe it's sky-diving, maybe it's a program like the one that once saw prisoners nurse neglected horses back to health at the Ferndale Institution near Mission. "It's that sort of program that the system needs to attract the drug addicts away from drugs."

It's also that sort of program that gets clean-living readers snarling and twisting their newspapers in rage. Skydiving? Horses? Club Fed? Decent working people can't afford to eat and this guy wants taxpayer-funded bungee-jumping for crackheads? Why not throw in geisha girls and a pass to Whistler, too?

But Frechette argued that unless you're prepared to shoot everyone convicted of a crime, or lock them up and throw away the key, unless you want them to make you a victim down the road, you had better do something to change them. "It's a choice between that and cutting them loose to recommit."

Which is exactly what happens. Recidivism is high.

Frechette himself was proof of what's wrong with the status quo, his story a variation on a theme repeated again and again. When he was a boy, his father taught him how to fight, how to shoplift. "My father led me to believe crime was okay as long as you don't get caught."

Drugs were okay, too. Frechette first used cocaine at fourteen when, with his father's permission, he did some that a family friend had brought to a party.

Frechette stayed straight for a while, working with horses at the Vancouver racetrack but turning to crack after losing his job at age twenty. "After a while, all you live for is the drugs."

Drifting around the Island and Lower Mainland, he'd do half a dozen burglaries a day. Jewellery, money, stereos—anything he could trade to a dealer for cocaine or cash. "Most of my break-and-enters were done in broad daylight."

He got caught now and then. Seven convictions for break-ins, a couple for possession of stolen property, plus theft, trafficking—during his twenties, he spent as much time in jail as out.

The threat of prison was no deterrent. He remembered a friend who did a string of armed robberies, all unmasked, all during the daytime, knowing he would get seven years when caught. He didn't care. "You don't care if you live or die, as long as you get that drug."

There was one time when Frechette turned himself in on an outstanding warrant, knowing that if he stayed on the street he'd wind up dead. Had someone approached him in prison at that point, offering a program that would replace the rush he got from cocaine and crime, "I would have jumped on it."

But all prison offered was Narcotics Anonymous meetings, which did nothing for him, and occasional access to heroin, which did.

Prison offered other lessons, though. When he first went inside, some guy looking for a little action told another inmate that Frechette had called that inmate an asshole. The inmate sucker-punched Frechette. "Are you going to take that dry?" asked other cons, wondering if Frechette would retaliate.

"Either you stand up for yourself, or everybody comes down on you." No choice but to be ruthless or be ostracized, turned into a punching bag.

Eighteen-year-olds, not yet old enough to buy cigarettes from the canteen, come in and get the hell beat out of them. By the time they emerge, the rest of us better watch out, because these guys are now angry and tough enough to do something about it.

"To put kids in with hardened criminals is ludicrous, because all they're doing is promoting violence."

On the day we met in 2000, Frechette said he had just met three or four "kids" at Wilkie who were ripe for having their lives turned around. But that's not what would happen.

"By simply throwing them in jail, all you're doing is introducing them to a darker side of life."

Many people argue that property crime would plunge if addicts didn't have to steal to support their habits. But Frechette opposed legalization, at least of harder drugs. "If they were to legalize cocaine or heroin, they'd be asking for trouble," he said. "They'd be giving people the right to commit suicide."

Get caught in the grip of drugs and your values go out the window, he said. Cocaine will drive you insane.

Something sure happened on that night in 1995, when Frechette stabbed Harris more than thirty times while at a party. The Crown said Frechette killed Harris to get the latter's cocaine. Frechette didn't deny that, but also said, "There was no reason for this murder."

"I was on cocaine and magic mushrooms at the time . . . That brought a demon out in me."

He said he was terrified by what he'd done and stopped using.

He said he was sorry for all his crimes, but particularly for killing Harris. "That's my biggest regret. I mean, this one cost a life. In a lot of ways, I would have preferred it to be my own."

So, here he sat in this little room in prison, right where you would expect a life of crime to leave him. Look back, and he saw regrets. Look ahead, and it was a life behind bars. "The world would be a better place if society started caring about the kids in time to save them, because there's a time at which it's too late unless that person runs into a brick wall. Like I did."

THAT INTERVIEW IN Wilkinson Road jail stayed with me over the years. In part, it was because of the grimness of the location. Prison can be brutal, the kind of place where, I was once told, guys will puke up their prescription methadone to sell for ten dollars a hit to other inmates—that is, if they don't get "heavied" into giving away the barfed-up drugs for free.

Mostly, the interview resonated because of Frechette himself. I had just interviewed the premier of the day, a man who had to weigh every word because to do otherwise would be political suicide. Frechette, by comparison, had nothing to gain and nothing to lose, so he just spoke his mind.

And when I tracked him down eighteen years later, in June 2018, he still did.

He was still in prison on that murder charge. He had bounced from institution to institution—Kent, Drumheller, William Head among them—before landing at medium-security Matsqui in the Fraser Valley. "I'm fifty years old and I've been in for twenty-three years," he said. "I'm completely institutionalized now."

That quitting drugs thing? The temptation eventually proved too strong. "It's pretty basic to get drugs in every institution," he said. They can have cameras pointing everywhere, listening devices, strip searches after visits—it still doesn't matter, the drugs pour in. "The staff do their best to control it and I give them kudos for that, but there's no way to stop the flow of drugs, inside or out."

But when we spoke, he had been clean again since 2010, which he thought would count for something when he applied for day parole in 2014. No, the parole board shot him down, said he still didn't understand his anger.

That felt like his one kick at the can, he said. He hasn't tried for day parole since. His next mandatory parole hearing isn't until 2021. "I'm at the point now where I've pretty much given up hope."

Frechette still feels the same way about turning young lives around, though. He has seen improvements, speaks positively about John Howard Society volunteers and a Victoria skills-for-recovery program that even includes kayaking and hiking for those on day parole. "That's the kind of thing you need," he says. Something to shine a little sunlight into hardened lives, show what's possible.

But the federal prison system is, at its core, unchanged, he says. "Basically, all they're doing is feeding guppies to the sharks."

He spoke of a twenty-two-year-old who had just got into a beef with another inmate over drugs. One way or another, the story wasn't going to end well. "This kid is definitely on a course where he's going to end up in a lot of trouble."

He sounded frustrated.

"The last thing I want to see is a kid like that end up a guy like me."

julie and colin angus

I'M A HERO. I have saved damsels in distress, pulled children from burning buildings, landed a jetliner after both pilot and co-pilot succumbed to simultaneous heart attacks (what are the odds!), and scored the Stanley Cup–winning goal.

I have wrestled razor-clawed grizzlies to give my family time to escape, packed an injured fellow climber down Everest, and, on one notable occasion, leapt in front of an assassin to take a bullet—fatally, as it turned out—that had been meant for the Queen.

Acceding to the pleas of an adoring public, I have appeared on television (Jimmy Fallon and Jimmy Kimmel had a tug-of-war over who would get me first) and downplayed my achievements in a charmingly self-deprecating manner. Of course, all this happened in my head while I was mowing the lawn or driving to work, but the daydreams did wonders for my ego.

Julie and Colin Angus, on the other hand, live out their dreams for real.

The Victoria couple are Canada's answer to Indiana Jones, or Thor Heyerdahl, or Lara Croft, or something like that. They have carved a career out of taking the rest of us along on vicarious adventures, challenging themselves with feats of physical endurance that they document in books and on film. In a paved and predictable world of office cubicles, uncalloused hands, and Groundhog Day traffic jams, their wilderness expeditions have enthralled those who crave the thrill, if not the hardship, of real-life exploration.

Colin, born in Victoria but raised with his three siblings in Port Alberni by their single mom, was the first to peer over the horizon. After high school, he and a buddy poured their savings into an eight-metre boat, took a three-day sailing course, and set out on what would become a five-year Pacific journey.

He burst into prominence in 2000 when, at age twenty-eight, he and two other young men—an Australian and a South African—spent five months crossing South America from coast to coast, in the process becoming the first people to ever raft the Amazon River from Andes to Atlantic. They started from the Pacific, climbing up, up, up to the top of the mountains along treacherous, rocky trails hacked from a bleak, windswept landscape as devoid of life as Oak Bay after dark. Then, from the first drops of melting snow that would become the Amazon, they plunged into the perils of the other side, enduring thirst, hunger, bugs, heat, cold, rapids, multiple capsizings, and even gunfire from Peruvian guerrillas.

In 2001 the same trio tackled the first source-to-sea descent of the 5,500-kilometre length of the world's fifth-longest river, the wild and remote Yenisei, which has its origins in the Hangayn Mountains of Mongolia and flows through Siberia to the Arctic Ocean. The gruelling, hair-raising trip included one twelve-day period in which Colin, separated from his companions, found himself alone in Mongolia with nothing but his pants, surviving on rhubarb and wild onions.

In 2004 began Colin's most gasp-worthy endeavour, the first human-powered circumnavigation of the globe—720 days, 43,000 kilometres, three continents, two oceans, and seventeen countries, all of it by ski, rowboat, bicycle, and foot. "It seemed like one of the last great challenges out there," he says. "The highest mountains had been climbed. The poles had been reached."

That's when Julie appeared on the scene—at least to the rest of us. With a master's degree in molecular biology from the University of Victoria, Colin's fiancée seemed cut out for a life in science but turned out to be an adventurer, too, setting out with Colin and another man as they began their journey. The three of them cycled the first 1,600 kilometres from Vancouver together, until Julie left the guys in Hyder, Alaska, as planned.

What wasn't planned were the conflicts that would see Colin and the other man split up in Siberia after paddling down the Yukon River and rowing across to Russia. Also unplanned were forest fires in Yukon, a vicious storm and near shipwreck in the Bering Sea, a run-in with a Russian grizzly, a frostbitten belly, Colin's hospitalization, day after day of bitter cold in the Siberian wilderness, and the Russian cops who stopped him as he cycled through the snow, then invited him into the back of the cop car to share their 9 AM moonshine.

"The closest I ever came to dying was when I was lost in Siberia and was stuck in a snow cave," he would later say. Minus forty-five, the wind howling, he didn't think he would last the night. But around two in the morning, the whiteout finally lifted, allowing Colin to see the lights of a settlement, so he kept going.

Julie joined him in Moscow and they cycled to Portugal. They then spent 156 days (pause to think about this) rowing from Europe to Central America, just the two of them cooped up in an eight-metre boat. That included a four-month stretch where they didn't once set foot on land—a stunning achievement for those of us who wouldn't blame our spouses for sticking a hatchet in our heads after the first three days.

"We were never farther apart than this," says Julie, spreading her arms. Along the way they got hit by two hurricanes ("I would have given anything to be anywhere else but there," she said), were almost run over by an onrushing freighter (their boat was flung aside by its bow wave), and came eyeball-to-eyeball with a great white shark the size of a small motorhome. Then, after a brief stop in the Caribbean, they spent another month rowing to Costa Rica, getting hammered by yet another storm. Julie, the first woman to row across the Atlantic, detailed it all in her book *Rowboat in a Hurricane*. For all this, National Geographic named the couple its adventurers of the year in 2006. And they still ended up getting married, too.

More adventures followed. In 2008 they took on Rowed Trip, a seven-month, 7,200-kilometre rowboat-and-bike journey from Colin's ancestral home at the top of Scotland to Syria, where Julie's father was born. They used their oars where they could, their folding bicycles and camping gear stowed in the boats that they designed and built themselves. Where the water was unnavigable, they towed the vessels behind the bikes—tough on the uphill, a little frightening on the down. They went through a lot of brake pads.

They endured hail, sleet, and snow in Scotland. Rowing through the heart of London, where they camped on a pontoon on Hammersmith Bridge, was awesome. Crossing the choppy English Channel offered more than a few heart-in-mouth moments. Someone swiped their trailer one night in a quiet lochside town in France, so they had to build another. Then came the Rhine in Germany, followed by the Danube all the way to the Black Sea. Some moments stood out: rowing through Budapest, all bridges and stately buildings; seeing a huge face carved into a mountainside in Romania; stumbling across a Black Sea shipwreck; sheltering on a Turkish beach for a couple of days, battered by a storm; and, finally, a joyful meeting with Julie's relatives at the Syrian farm where the family had grown olives for three hundred years.

That spawned their next great adventure. After a solo adventure for Colin—a record-breaking effort in which he rowed his way around Vancouver Island in record time, completing the 1,150-kilometre circumnavigation inside fifteen days, twelve hours—the couple took on Olive Odyssey, a 2011 sailing trip through the centuries-old trading routes of the Mediterranean (read Julie's book on the subject, a deep dive into the history and culture of olive farming, and you will never want to buy inferior olive oil again).

By that time son Leif had arrived. He was, as you might expect, an active baby, colic giving his parents plenty of sleep-deprivation time to ponder the consequences of passing on adventurers' genes.

"There are a few nights when I think I would change motherhood for being in the rowboat," Julie said from their home in the Comox Valley. "Rowing across the Atlantic was good training for parenthood."

The sailboat was their concession to parenthood. "We had to think of a trip that would allow him to travel safely," Julie said. Leif was not yet one year old when the Anguses embarked on a journey that they planned to finish at Julie's family's olive farm.

Except they never got there. Before they could reach Syria, war broke out—leading to the Anguses' most-ambitious project ever: the struggle to bring Julie's family to safety in Canada.

It seems almost absurd, given everything the couple had been through, that they didn't even have to leave Vancouver Island for their greatest adventure of all. Long before the rest of Canada was galvanized to respond to a struggle that seemed so distant, so abstract, to many of us, the Anguses were trying to ease the pain of Syria. Julie was particularly active. Even as the Anguses packed up for a move to Victoria in 2013, Julie was fundraising to buy medicine for an Iraqi relief camp where eighty thousand Syrians, mostly under ten years of age, were crammed into a place built for twelve thousand.

Mostly, she feared for her father's brother, Bassam Wafai, his wife, Alia, and their three children. The war was hard on the Wafais. In 2014, the only other family still living in their Aleppo apartment building was killed by a falling bomb. The family stayed in the damaged building until things got so bad that they could stay no longer. In March 2015 they paid a smuggler and made the dangerous border crossing to Turkey. There they languished in a country in which they were barely tolerated.

Julie desperately wanted to help them get out, but Ottawa wasn't particularly interested in welcoming Syrian refugees. That changed in the autumn of 2015, after photos of three-year-old Alan Kurdi, who drowned with his five-year-old brother and their mother while trying to flee the conflict, roused a somnolent world. It was Victoria-based journalist Terry Glavin who found the Canadian link to the story, a Coquitlam relative with shattered dreams of bringing the

Kurdi family to Canada. (Those deaths affected the Anguses, whose own boys—they had a second son, Oliver, in 2014—were of a similar age.) After that, Ottawa vowed to fast-track 25,000 Syrians to Canada.

Dozens of Vancouver Island groups were among those who emerged to sponsor newcomers. In Victoria, the Anguses were at the nucleus of sixteen Fairfield residents who came together to sponsor the Wafais. They quickly raised the $55,000 needed to sustain the family during their first year in Canada. Two members of the sponsoring group, both University of Victoria professors, donated a suite in their home.

Then Julie, Colin, the profs, and the rest of the sponsors waited and waited for the red tape to be cut, not knowing when (or if) the Wafais would arrive. Frustration set in. "It's been eight years since I last saw them in their home in Syria," Julie said in 2016. Even as other Syrians streamed onto Vancouver Island, the Wafais remained stuck in Turkey.

It was ironic, then, that after all that waiting, neither of the Anguses was in town when the Syrians finally made it to Victoria that July. Colin was up north, having just become the first solo rower (most entrants compete as teams) to complete that year's gruelling, two-week Race to Alaska from Port Townsend, Washington, to Ketchikan, a stunning feat of grit and endurance. Julie was on the mainland, committed to appearing in a car commercial with television's Survivorman, Les Stroud.

She did manage to cross paths with the Wafais at the Vancouver airport, though. There was a special moment when a stranger rushed up to welcome them, too. It was a nice introduction to Canada for refugees who hadn't exactly been embraced with open arms in Turkey. "I think that's a feeling they haven't had," Julie said.

Bassam confirmed that. The Wafais had had their hopes dashed so many times, had suffered so many setbacks, that even after being told the family was coming to Canada that week, he didn't believe it. "We will stay in this prison forever," he told himself.

Once in Victoria, it felt as if they were emerging from a nightmare. "We can't believe ourselves. Are we in paradise?" asked Bassam a couple of days after arriving. The fine artist speaks fluent English, but on that day was having trouble expressing the depth of his gratitude to those who brought his family to Canada. "There's a future here for my daughters, my children," he said. "There are human rights here."

As he spoke, daughters Rawan, eleven, and Toulip, fifteen, beamed like sunshine. No, he said, they didn't do that before arriving in Canada. Asked for her favourite moment so far, Rawan (nicknamed Nemo because she once had naturally striped hair reminiscent of the Disney fish) spoke of being greeted by their sponsors at the airport. Toulip said landing in Victoria was like landing on the moon—and it turns out the moon is a totally awesome place. It was hard not to look at them, absolutely radiating happiness, without thinking of how close they had come to remaining trapped in a totally different life.

The Wafais eventually moved to Toronto, where son Nour was aiming to go to flight school, but the Anguses and their Fairfield sponsorship group weren't done. In 2017 they were at the Victoria airport to welcome Maz Al-Wafai, a twenty-five-year-old Syrian software developer whose last name indicated he may have been related to Julie. Even if he wasn't, it sure felt like he was. The rest of the sponsors felt like family, too, he said, the year after his arrival.

"Their emotional support, just the fact that you can lean on someone, that someone has your back, is something I haven't felt in a while," he said.

In April 2018, Al-Wafai was joined in Victoria by his brother, his sister, and her two young children, who had been stranded in Turkey after enduring the war in Syria. It was the first time the siblings had all been together in eight years.

Their story, and that of the Wafais, offered proof of what ordinary people like those in the Fairfield group can do when they choose to make a difference. "It makes me smile at the beauty of humanity and how wonderful people can be," Julie said after her uncle's arrival.

It was a reminder of a conversation I had had with Colin and Julie years earlier, when asking about the difference between them and the Walter Mitty dreamers for whom, in real life, adventure means nothing riskier than driving to the ferry terminal without a reservation. (Actually, what I said was, "Why is it that a select few of us are able to seize the reins of life, while others only ride fantasies?")

Both insisted they were nothing special, that their feats were just a matter of determination. "Perseverance is what it's all about," Colin said. "Neither Julie nor myself have any God-given skills."

The hardest part of adventuring, they maintain, is the first step. "All you have to say," says Colin, "is 'I'm going to do it.'"

the fort street
refugees

HIEP NGUYEN NEARLY drowned in the storm. There were seventy-five of them crammed in a boat just twenty feet long. They had pooled their gold for a chance to escape Vietnam.

Six days, seven nights it took to reach the Philippines, except on one of those nights a howling gale almost put them under. No lifejackets, so they clung to bits of Styrofoam as waves swamped their open craft.

"Very much scary, almost died," Nguyen says.

He's sitting at a table in his Pho Vy Vietnamese Restaurant at 772 Fort Street in Victoria, tracing the thread that pulled him to Canada as a refugee more than a quarter century ago.

Next door at the Brothers Barbershop, at 770 Fort, Visar and Artor Gashi have their own refugee tale. Forcibly expelled from their native Kosovo during the war with Serbia in 1999, they built a life in Canada after being plucked from a camp in Macedonia.

What are the odds: two refugee-run small businesses right next to each other in downtown Victoria.

Their owners have little else in common. Different ages, different languages, came here at different times from home-lands half a world apart—but they share a profound sense of gratitude to their adoptive country. On Canada Day, nobody is prouder of Canada than Nguyen and the Gashi brothers. Others among us might take what we have for granted. Not them.

This is a nation of immigrants. One in five of us was born elsewhere. Even if you're native-born, odds are your grandparents have an accent from somewhere else. But actual refugees—those driven here by warfare or persecution—make up a tiny slice of the immigrant pie.

Our history as a safe haven predates Canada itself. Loyalists fleeing the American Revolution migrated here in the late eighteenth century. So did Scots chased out by the Highland Clearances.

A quarter million refugees arrived after the Second World War. More than 37,000 Hungarians flooded in after the failed uprising of 1956 and 11,000 Czechs after the Prague Spring turned to winter in 1968. The 1970s saw post-Allende Chileans, Bengali Muslims uprooted by the war in Bangladesh, and Ugandan Asians ousted by Idi Amin.

Prior to the influx of Syrians—something like 50,000 of them since 2015, Julie Angus's relatives included—the most celebrated intake was when Canada embraced more than 60,000 Vietnamese boat people around 1980.

Nguyen arrived a few years after that wave. In 1987, he was twenty-two years old, working for the Vietnamese railway and going nowhere fast. He wanted to get ahead in life, but the authorities blunted his education and job opportunities, punishing his family for its past; Nguyen's father had been a dentist in the South Vietnamese army. So bleak was his future that a risky escape to the Philippines and, he hoped, the United States seemed the best option. He left the coastal city of Nha Trang with the blessing of a family that included his new bride and a newborn son. "Eight years I don't see him," he says. "Very lonely. Very sad."

The boat slipped into the sea in darkness, at 3 AM. No one had luggage. The passengers had abandoned their packs after the authorities, suspicious that something was afoot, began busting anyone found with baggage. That meant that although Nguyen survived the crossing, he had nothing but the clothes on his back during his two years in a Philippine refugee camp.

One day, when Nguyen was volunteering in the camp library, a Canadian government official borrowed a book, then asked if Nguyen would like to come here. Canada? Nguyen barely knew where it was on the map.

They sent him to Saskatchewan in 1989, but the minus-fifty-five wind chill blew him to Victoria a few months later. He lived at the capital's Buddhist temple as he started the long, hard climb up the ladder typical of so many immigrants: $2.50-an-hour janitor, then restaurant dishwasher, then, after training at Camosun College, chef. In 1995, he was finally reunited with his wife and son in Victoria.

Nguyen cooked at the Japanese Village restaurant for several years before opening his own place, Pho Vy, in 2003. It's open seven days a week. He rarely takes a day off. His wife and children (the couple have a Canadian-born daughter) work there, too.

Next door, the Gashi brothers opened their business in 2015. They're pretty proud of the place, having branched out on their own after working down the block at Jimmy's, another immigrant-owned barbershop, for most of their time in the BC capital.

The brothers were already barbers when Artor, then nineteen, and Visar, then twenty-one, arrived in Victoria in 1999, two of the five thousand Kosovar refugees taken in by Canada during a dramatic emergency airlift that year. Visar—you can call him Vic—had been the first to take up the trade, turning to hair-cutting after Albanian-speaking Kosovars saw their schools shut down in the unrest leading up to the war to break away from Yugoslavia. By the time full-on fighting broke out in 1998, Artor was a barber, too.

They cut hair while also volunteering for the Mother Teresa humanitarian organization in the capital, Pristina. After being forced from Kosovo by Yugoslav president Slobodan Milosevic's regime, they cut hair in their refugee camp in Macedonia, too (buzz cuts only, because of the lice).

It was in Macedonia that they got a positive impression of Canada. They liked the professional way Canada's peacekeepers —part of the NATO force that waded in after Milosevic's mass expulsions—handled themselves. "It was a well-educated army," Visar says. He wanted his kids to grow up in a country that produced soldiers like that.

By then, family was on Visar's mind. He had been walking around with an engagement ring for months, planning to propose to his girlfriend, Edita, once peace returned. But with no sign of the conflict abating, he finally popped the question as the war raged on.

"I didn't want to die with the ring in my pocket," he says.

By 2018 Visar and Edita had three teenagers growing up in Canada, just like he wanted. Artor and his wife have two children of their own. They're all-Canadian families now, eager to be part of the community. They're so happy, so proud, to throw a Cops for Cancer fundraiser each year.

Ask the brothers what stands out nineteen years after being taken in by Canada, and they say it's the welcome they got.

"We started feeling at home right away," Artor says.

"We didn't expect that much respect," says his big brother. "When we came here, they made us feel like special people."

Next door, their fellow refugee Hiep Nguyen is eager—really eager—to finally get the opportunity to express his gratitude. He says he remains overwhelmed by the kindness he has met.

"I want to say thank you to all Canadians for giving me a chance," he says, touching his heart.

The stoicism slips away. He chokes up. "I feel very, very lucky to stay in Canada."

More than 20 million refugees are adrift in the world today. On Fort Street, some of them know they won the lottery.

glass ball fever

"UP ALL NIGHT," read Barry Campbell's log entry for April 14, 1987. "Glass ball fever."

He found thirty-six Japanese fishing floats that time, a personal record. Made a trail of them for wife Barb to follow in the morning.

Had to earn his bonanza, though. Leaned into the teeth of a howling rainstorm not long before midnight and trudged Long Beach, twelve kilometres each way, scouring the shoreline. Went through four flashlights picking his way through the washed-up bull kelp, packing crates, shoes, and other tempest-tossed jetsam.

When he finally got back home with his treasures, it was time to stagger off to work at the national park's interpretive centre, a sight that must have alarmed the tourists. "I felt I was radioactive because I was glowing so much from the windburn," he recalled. "I was bright red."

For this, dear reader, is the brutal beachcombing truth: if you want glass balls, you need an iron will. While the open ocean tosses all manner of unexpected marvels onto the sands of Vancouver Island's west coast, the competition to find the waterborne wonders is as fierce as the weather that drives them ashore.

Anyone who has trod an empty stretch of sand has entertained dreams of exotic discoveries: a message in a bottle, perhaps, or a volleyball named Wilson, or a floating foot (okay, maybe not a foot, though those do bob up from time to time).

Barry Campbell wasn't just a beachcomber, of course. After he passed away in 2016, he was remembered as an ardent naturalist and outdoorsman, and as a devoted community volunteer in Tofino—but it was the beachcombing that appealed to the Robinson Crusoe lurking within deskbound city-dwellers.

"It's the excitement and mystery of finding something that's come from so far away, something that's got a story behind it," said Barbara Campbell one day in 2008, eyeing a selection of ocean offerings outside their Tofino home.

One of the Campbells' deck chairs was found on a beach. So was their snow shovel. "My laundry basket that I've used for twenty-five years is beachcombed," Barbara said. They had found downhill skis, sleds, even three worse-for-wear televisions on one day.

Most cherished of all by serious beachcombers are Japanese fishing floats. The glass balls are no longer used by the deep-sea fleet, but they still drift in, rare as a Trumpian truth. Some are the size of apples, others as big as beach balls. Spheres, cylinders, rolling pins—most have the greenish hue of the recycled sake bottles from which they were made, but some are amber or blue. Many are etched with their manufacturer's mark. "Some of these could be sixty, seventy years old," Barry said, examining the collection on his deck.

You can actually sniff out a good beachcombing tide, one where the telltale odour of rotting seaweed and other flotsam is carried on the south winds hammering in from the open ocean. "It smells like glass balls are coming in," Barry would say.

That's when you bundle up head to toe in full rubber rain gear and head out into the elements to be the first on the scene. If another beachcomber's car is already in the parking lot, give up and go elsewhere. "We call that the glass ball Olympics, when people are dashing here and there to get to a beach."

"If you're really dedicated, you stay up all night," he said. That means wading rivers in the dark or contending with wolves patrolling the shoreline for dead birds and other creatures washed in by the storm. Some beachcombers use inflatable rafts to cross creeks, while others even use float planes to reach remote locations.

Oak Bay–raised Barry got the beachcombing bug as a boy on outings to French Beach and Port Renfrew with his dad. Never found much, but the possibilities fired his imagination. It was in 1965, as eighteen-year-olds hiking the West Coast Trail, that he and two University of Victoria buddies were each given a pair of Japanese fishing floats by the Pachena Point lighthouse keeper, who had found the glass balls that morning.

Barry's own first find was in 1967, a five-inch ball picked up off Mabens Beach, facing Pachena Bay. He picked up his 336th glass ball (actually, that includes forty or so found by Barb and their boys, Mike and Ben) in 2010.

By then he had spent forty years in Tofino, arriving in 1970 as the fifth person hired to work in what became the Pacific Rim National Park Reserve. He retired in 2002 (at least in theory; he later put in thousands of volunteer hours clearing the park of broom and other invasive species), which allowed more time for the Campbells to poke into out-of-the-way places. They would boat over to Flores Island, Vargas Island, and other places whose beaches are off the beaten path.

Not many fishing floats wash ashore these days. They're a relic of the past. See a glass ball today, it's likely to be a tourist trinket that arrived on a cargo ship, not a storm-pushed tide. (You can tell the difference: the replicas are unweathered, made of thinner glass, often bound in unworn rope.)

Lots of other stuff comes in, though. Langford-raised Barbara spotted a mannequin once, a US Coast Guard rescue dummy clothed in a survival suit, partly hidden in the driftwood on Vargas Island. At first, she feared it was alive—or, worse, not alive.

All manner of odd bits show up: in the early 1970s it was Transonics electronics, made for the old Woodward's department stores, that showed up on West Coast Trail beaches, having somehow been dislodged in transit. Drift cards, tossed in the water by oceanographers tracking currents, are picked up, then mailed back to their source, often places in California or Washington State. In 1985, a flotilla of packing boxes came bobbing ashore, each containing five hundred graham wafer–sized sheets of California redwood that had escaped while being shipped to Japan to be made into pencils. In 2011, Barry said he had been finding walnuts and almonds that had washed out of groves and down the Sacramento River and elsewhere in central California.

Barry also picked up eighty or ninety Nikes, part of a shipment of eighty thousand that famously washed off a ship off Alaska in 1990. Not just runners, but hiking shoes, too. They were strewn up and down the west coast of the Island, residents picking them up, trying to swap with each other for a matching pair. "I think I got one pair of light hikers that were a match," Barry said. Some people had hundreds of shoes.

Alas, some of the footwear had been in the water long enough to have goose barnacles growing on it, and when the barnacles died, well, the Nikes smelled gnarly. "They were pretty stinky," Barry said. Ditto for the Italian sandals that washed up in the early 1990s. They came in either grey or fluorescent blue, with an air cushion in the sole. "I got dozens of them."

The Campbells once came across brick-sized plastic emergency kits designed for Japanese-shipwreck victims, each kit crammed with packages of food ("The Japanese seed cakes, they were really good," Barbara said) and a note reading "Never give up! Rescue is coming!"

Barry's coolest find was in 1987, while he was walking Chesterman Beach. He saw a pop bottle, ignored it at first, then decided to backtrack and pick it up, curious as to why its cap had been taped shut. He used tweezers to extract what turned out to be a note from Katano Elementary School in Osaka, Japan. A letter to the school elicited a blizzard of replies from its students, mostly in Japanese, which the Campbells had translated by Tofino's pharmacist. The students explained that they had celebrated the school's centennial by launching twenty-eight bottles in 1985; only Barry's was found. Also in the bottle were what appeared to be a few small pebbles, but were in fact seeds; one grew into an odd-smelling houseplant that proved a source of curiosity until it died. Barry ended up being interviewed for Japanese television by John Gathright, a Victoria-raised man who had become a well-known media personality in Japan. (Who knew?)

If some finds are the product of midnight foul-weather sleuthing in remote locations, others drop—or float—in like manna from heaven, most often when cargo has been swept off passing freighters.

Barbara recalls Tofitians swarming Chesterman Beach after a shipping container of cedar shake blocks spilled its contents. Residents were trotting off the sand with full wheelbarrows, only to trot back again on the orders of the RCMP, who said the rightful owners were coming. But when no one appeared to collect the shake blocks, back came the wheelbarrows.

Then there was the time a stainless steel refrigerated shipping container washed ashore. Tofitians rubbed their hands in eager anticipation, wondering what treasure could be inside. It was—ta-da!—salal, bear grass, and evergreen huckleberry, bound for florists in New Zealand. To Tofino, it was coals to Newcastle. What a letdown.

Much more welcome is the lumber that occasionally gets washed overboard. "Some people basically built their houses with it," Barry said. Snoop behind some Tofino homes and you might find some of the mahogany—two-metre-long lengths of rough-cut four-by-fours—that floated in.

The most celebrated scavenger hunt came in 1972 after the 144-metre cargo ship *Vanlene* plowed into Austin Island in Barkley Sound, which its captain had—oops!—mistaken for Juan de Fuca Strait. The ship was carrying 300 brand new Dodge Colts, 131 of which were salvaged by helicopter. After that, it was open season, the stricken ship swarmed by people who boated over from Tofino, Ucluelet, and Bamfield. They made off with lifeboats, linen, tools, doors, furniture—anything they could, including engines pulled out of the Colts. Alas, being made of pot metal, the engines didn't last long in the damp West Coast.

Barry climbed the ship's ladder to get on board. More than a quarter century later, he could still remember the sound of the water sloshing inside the hull: "It was really eerie." At one point, he slipped on the oil-slicked deck, but managed to grab a rail before sliding into the chuck. He rescued a variety of items that now rest in the national park archives: the ship's log, some Japanese editions of *Reader's Digest*. As for the *Vanlene*, it broke in two and slid to the bottom, where it became popular among scuba divers.

One of the most sensational beach finds was made by Haida Gwaii's Peter Mark in 2012. Half-buried in a remote Graham Island beach was a Harley-Davidson motorcycle that had bobbed across the Pacific in a Styrofoam-packed container after Japan's devastating earthquake and tsunami in March 2011. Ralph Tieleman, a long-haired, Harley-loving Tofitian (and art collector, whose collection includes works by Emily Carr, Tom Thomson, and Arthur Lismer) picked up the bike from Mark in Prince Rupert and brought it to Steve Drane's motorcycle shop in Victoria, where it looked like the worst garage sale find ever: spokes busted, seat gone, gas tank full of sand, rocks jammed against the crankcase. The restored 2004 Night Train was eventually shipped to the Harley-Davidson Museum in Wisconsin at the request of its Japanese owner.

Unfortunately, much of what does float in these days is unwanted, even toxic: the billions of tiny pieces of plastic garbage that litter the sand. "We call it beach confetti," Barry said. Some of it comes in the form of the pill-sized pellets that are the base material for just about anything made of plastic. Some of it is simply trash, broken down and degraded over time—perhaps it has spun away from the Great Pacific Garbage Patch, the swirling mid-ocean mess that in March 2018 was estimated to be three times the size of France.

The plastic bits shimmer in the sun when it catches them in the foaming tip of a wave. "There are places where it's absolutely spectacular," Barry said. "It's very colourful. In some places it comprises a tremendous portion of the surface area of the sand." It's also death for the birds and fish that eat it, mistaking it for food.

This isn't just a Vancouver Island problem, of course. Anywhere the earth meets the water, garbage abounds.

But for those who know when and where to look, there's also treasure.

rudi

THE ATOMIC BOMB detonated over Nagasaki at 11:02 AM.

Rudi Hoenson didn't see the B-29 that dropped it—"We were not allowed to stand and look at things"—but he heard it.

The plane droned overhead as Hoenson and his fellow prisoners of war laboured to clear the rubble left by an earlier conventional air raid, one that had killed the man sheltering next to him.

This time, death arrived without warning. Hoenson caught a quick glimpse of something coming down by parachute. Then . . .

"It was a blinding flash." A blast of hot air slammed the twenty-two-year-old Dutchman to the ground.

His legs were burned, but he was relatively lucky. Two metres away, three men who had been pushing a cart were badly hurt, their clothes on fire. Wooden buildings, slapped down by an unseen hand, were engulfed in flames. Gas cylinders exploded. The noise, heat, and smoke were overwhelming. Confusion reigned. "It was a scene of death and dying."

The prisoners, all of them burned, some so severely that they had to be carried by the others, headed for what they hoped was safety. Crossing a canal, they picked their way through the flaming remains of a densely packed residential area, one where the men had all gone to work for the day, leaving their families behind.

Everywhere Hoenson looked, there were Japanese women and children, their clothes ripped apart, their faces and bodies bleeding. He remembers a baby clinging to its dead mother. Nearby, another mother cried as she held a gravely injured little girl. Several people had been blinded by the flash. The fires were getting worse.

"I wished there was something I could do for them, especially the children. I wondered how long it would take before they could get any help. Think of it—the whole city was flattened."

It took Hoenson until 2015, the seventieth anniversary of the Nagasaki bomb, to relate this story. At age ninety-two, he had never told it before.

HERE'S THE RUDI HOENSON we knew before he opened up: much-loved, much-admired Victoria philanthropist who had given millions to local charities.

Here's the version he kept to himself: survivor of the only nuclear war mankind has known.

Ask him why he never talked about it before and he squirms a little, grimaces. Maybe he didn't want to sound like he was showing off, he says. He was, in truth, reluctant to tell his story even at ninety-two, wondering what good would be done by telling the tale.

The good, replies his friend Jennifer Jasechko, comes from the rest of the story: how a man—a boy, really—can witness unspeakable depravity, endure three and a half years of brutal captivity, be starved to the point of death, and live through the horror of nuclear war, yet emerge with his soul intact, his heart free of bitterness.

It was Jasechko, who worked with the aging veterans at Broadmead Lodge—one of Hoenson's favourite causes—who coaxed many of the details from him.

His story goes back to December 1941, when Japan invaded oil-rich Indonesia, then known as the Dutch East Indies. Hoenson, an eighteen-year-old whose architect father had been sent out from the Netherlands, joined a small, ill-equipped defence force that stubbornly resisted for a few days before being overwhelmed. Taken captive, he spent three months in Singapore's notorious Changi Prison before being herded into a small rustbucket of a ship—two hundred men crammed in the hold, one ventilation shaft, stifling heat, everyone deathly ill with dysentery—and sent to Japan.

They ended up in Nagasaki's prisoner-of-war camp Fukuoka 14. Life there was harsh, the prisoners treated with contempt, beaten by their Japanese guards. "In their culture, we should not have surrendered," Hoenson says. "In their eyes, we were nothing." On one occasion, not bowing to the satisfaction of a soldier earned him a rifle butt to the mouth, costing him five teeth—three upper, two lower—but he says they were rotten and ready to go anyway.

Food was scarce, though Hoenson points out that by the end of the Second World War, the Japanese were starving, too. Hoenson, who went into the camp at about 170 pounds, weighed less than 80 when freed.

The 534 prisoners at Fukuoka 14 had been sent to Nagasaki as slave labour. Hoenson found himself an arc welder in the Mitsubishi shipyard, standing on a two-by-twelve plank seven storeys in the air while constructing a fifty thousand–tonne aircraft carrier. Prisoners worked ten hours a day, 362 days a year—they got two days off at New Year's and one for the emperor's birthday.

After the Allied blockade starved the shipyard of building materials, the prisoners were split into two groups. About 170 were sent to the coal mines at Mukden, while the remaining 200 (Hoenson estimates more than 160 had died in captivity by then) went to work in a foundry across from the prison. Hoenson, in the latter group, found himself welding gun turrets for smaller vessels. It was there, during an August 1, 1945, air raid, that a bomb landed within ten metres of his shelter, killing the man beside him and leaving Hoenson with a head wound that took sixteen stitches to close, without anaesthetic.

The prisoners were clearing rubble from the ruined foundry when the atomic bomb exploded on August 9, 1945.

The plutonium-based device, nicknamed Fat Man, was carried in an American B-29 Superfortress called *Bockscar*. Nagasaki, a city of a quarter million—smaller than Greater Victoria—wasn't *Bockscar*'s primary target. The bomb was supposed to be dropped on Kokura. But with that city obscured by cloud and smoke, fuel running low, and anti-aircraft fire getting close, the aircraft shifted to the secondary target: Nagasaki.

At 11 AM, an accompanying B-29 dropped blast-measuring instruments by parachute; this must be what Hoenson glimpsed.

Then the bomb was dropped, exploding five hundred metres over Nagasaki, generating heat measured at 3,900°C and winds of 1,005 kilometres an hour.

Estimates of the number who died that day vary widely, from 22,000 to 80,000. The most common figure used is 40,000, with a similar number succumbing in the following days and months.

The toll would have been even higher had *Bockscar*'s bombardier, peering through the clouds on an overcast day, not dropped the weapon more than two kilometres off-target. Hoenson read later that the bombardier mistook the outlying Urakami railway station for the central Nagasaki depot, which had a similar appearance. The Urakami district, not the more densely populated city centre, became Ground Zero.

The mistake saved Hoenson's life. Instead of being seven hundred metres from the hypocentre of the blast, he was fifteen hundred metres away—just far enough for a chance to survive.

The Fukuoka 14 prisoners had no idea what could have caused such a massive explosion. They didn't know another nuclear weapon had fallen on Hiroshima three days earlier. "I thought, 'My gosh, they must have developed a big bomb,'" Hoenson says. "For days, we didn't know what it was."

They knew it had turned Nagasaki into a raging, burning hell, though, with an apocalyptic mushroom column towering over the destruction below. Hoenson suggested seeking shelter beyond some far hills. It took four hours for thirty of the prisoners, many of them injured, to cover four or five kilometres, working through the narrow passages between wood-frame buildings that were going up like kindling. Progress was slowed by the need to carry two badly wounded men. One, named Van der Meulen, had been a high school teacher. The other, a doctor's son named Hans Krol, was burned down his entire left side. They were Hoenson's best friends.

The flames receded as they moved, though it seemed odd that the crops in the fields had wilted. Met by Japanese soldiers, they were stuffed into a small police station where they could only sit, not lie down. They were parched, but there was no water. Two wooden buckets of rice arrived that evening, but the POWs had to pick broken glass out of it before eating. Krol in particular was in bad shape. "I held him like a baby all night long, poor guy," Hoenson says.

The next morning, Hoenson's urine was the colour of black coffee, with a reddish tint. "We did not know why at the time, but now realize it was due to radiation."

Months later, the effects still showed. "Pieces came out when I combed my hair, and I had trouble with my eyesight."

Later, there were stories of radiation victims' offspring being born with severe deformities. "Two army doctors ordered me not to have children, because of the radiation I received." It was because of that, many years on, that Hoenson and his wife decided not to have children of their own.

Once out of the police station, the POWs were herded into a larger group of prisoners and spent three days foraging for food and water—in the radiation zone. Some tore their shirts for others to use as bandages. The eighty healthiest prisoners used salvaged doors and ladders to carry the twenty who couldn't walk.

On the fourth morning, the relatively healthy ones were sent back into the devastation to retrieve the Japanese dead. "Being the fourth day in the heat, some corpses started to bloat and smell. We dragged the remains to an open field for identification. By the end of the day, we all smelled like dead bodies."

The next day it got worse. Among the victims were dozens of young women who had died when the big rice- and soup-cookers of an industrial-scale kitchen toppled on them. The Dutchmen had to be careful not to pull limbs off the bodies they moved with their bare hands.

More of the same followed until, one day at noon, the prisoners were ordered back to camp. The war, they were told, was over. Japan surrendered on August 15.

Hoenson's excitement was short-lived. "I was too tired and all I wanted was to lie down and rest." He estimates another twenty prisoners died in the month before the Yanks arrived. Many more died later on the hospital ship USS *Haven*.

On September 15, the freed POWs were moved to Nagasaki's harbour, where they were treated to hot showers and new US Marine uniforms. "Oh, that felt so nice," Hoenson says. "For three and a half years, I never had a bath or any clothes that fit." New underwear to replace the Japanese strap-and-string thing? Luxury.

So was all the chicken and steak that the Americans prepared for them. Their liberators also laid out tables of toiletries, books, watches, and more, all free for the taking. "But most of us were too timid after not getting anything for so long, and we were just too intimidated to grab the presents."

After that came the long journey home and the even-slower journey back to health. Hoenson remained sick in post-war Holland, sapped of energy, contracting pneumonia. In 1950, he wrote to the US government, asking to be tested for after-effects of the atomic bomb, but nothing came of it.

It wasn't until he emigrated that his life turned a corner. He had been given the choice between the US and Canada, but picked the latter because of the classic movie *Rose Marie*, featuring Jeanette MacDonald as an opera singer and Nelson Eddy as a Mountie riding a horse through the wilderness. "It looked so beautiful and interesting."

Hoenson arrived in 1951 with fifty dollars in his pocket. On his second day in Calgary, he got a job as a geological draftsman. Catching the beginning of the oil boom, he worked hard and plowed his savings into what turned out to be smart investments. Best of all, he met a Saskatchewan-raised teacher, Sylvia Mae, the love of his life. They wedded in 1956, moved to Victoria in 1979.

"Coming to Canada was wonderful for me," he once said, "but meeting Sylvia was the main reason I recovered."

They travelled the world extensively (including one adventure that included a wonderful few days in Japan) before age and infirmity caught up, whereupon they turned to philanthropy. Their first donation—$20,000 to the Victoria Foundation—launched the Rudi and Sylvia Hoenson Foundation. After Sylvia suffered a slight stroke, a $55,000 gift brought a piece of stroke detection equipment to Royal Jubilee Hospital in 2004. When she had a leg problem, a $25,000 gift let the Queen Alexandra Centre for Children's Health establish a gait lab for children with mobility problems.

It was after Sylvia died in 2008 that Rudi began divesting himself of most of "a small pile of money." Among the donations were $1 million to the Victoria Hospital Foundation, $400,000 for a CT scanner and operating rooms at Saanich Peninsula Hospital, another $400,000 to BC Children's Hospital and the Queen Alexandra Centre, and $350,000 for BC Cancer Foundation research.

By 2016 the Veterans Memorial Lodge at Broadmead, home to many of his fellow veterans, had received $1 million of the millions he had given away. Hoenson shrugged off his generosity. "At my age, what else are you going to do? I ask everybody to find me a nice thirty-nine-year-old girl, but no one can find one. I must be difficult, or something."

The honours poured in. In 2013, he received the Generosity of Spirit Award at Vancouver Island's National Philanthropy

Day awards. Victoria's Government House unveiled Rudi's Tea Room in recognition of his efforts. Saanich's Reynolds Secondary—whose staff and students he joined in shaving his head for the Tour de Rock cancer fundraiser—celebrated him at a ceremony. In April 2018, one of Judith Guichon's last acts as BC's lieutenant-governor was to present him with a vice-regal commendation.

In late 2016, the Netherlands' military attaché to Canada flew out from Ottawa to (somewhat belatedly, Hoenson pointed out) pin a couple of medals on him. That might have been an olive branch: earlier that year Hoenson had bristled when the Dutch government sent him €25,000—roughly $36,000—as compensation for wages lost during captivity. It came way too late for the former Dutch POWs who could have used the money but had since died, he says. He wrote a rocket of a letter to the Dutch government, chastising it for not making the widows and heirs of the dead prisoners eligible for the payments. "Under no circumstances would I use that money for my own pleasure," he says. Hoenson gave the money to the Lodge at Broadmead.

Now well into his nineties, he still carries himself with an easy, good-humoured self-confidence. If his hearing is fading, his mind remains sharp. He still lives alone, drives a car, and does his own cooking because he loves to eat well—a legacy of the three and a half years of near-starvation. "In the camp, we never talked about women. It was always food we talked about."

Those times will never leave him. On the contrary, he says he thinks back to the war more frequently as he ages.

"Bad dreams come more often," he says. He can't shake the memory of the particularly savage killing of two Dutch prisoners, one that the rest of the captives were forced to watch. He has nightmares about the atomic aftermath, too: "The fires, heat, smoke, burned bodies, women and children with open wounds, their flesh hanging loose, ripped apart by the blast, total confusion, no help. I was there and experienced it all and I wonder if this is an example awaiting us sinners in hell."

What is truly remarkable, given all this, is his lack of anger. He is not bitter. He does not dwell. "You get on with things. Coming to Canada, meeting Sylvia—what else do you want?" He bears no ill will toward the Japanese, who he says acted according to the dictates of what was then their way of thinking.

"I don't have any hard feelings. It was part of their upbringing, part of their culture that we were nobodies." The officers ordered the soldiers to be rough on the prisoners, and the soldiers complied.

The guards themselves weren't spared. "We got slapped, but if a Japanese soldier did something wrong, his officer would slap him just like us."

Nor is he bitter toward those who unleashed the atomic bomb—though it does bother him that the Americans never admitted they knew the Fukuoka 14 POW camp was in the blast zone when they decided to drop it. "Were they ashamed that they dropped the bomb on us? They shouldn't be." Nagasaki was a legitimate military target, crowded with shipyards and factories, he says. "I have not complained about them doing the bombing. My only complaint is they did not acknowledge there were two hundred prisoners of war."

Some might be surprised that he supported the decision to drop the atomic bomb on Nagasaki, even after seeing the horror. The alternative, he says, was worse: a drawn-out slaughter that may have killed 2 million people before Japan surrendered. He points to the March 1945 firebombing of Tokyo by three hundred planes, a raid that killed between 80,000 and 130,000 civilians. On his way home from captivity, Hoenson flew out of Okinawa in the nose of a B-29 bomber. It offered a bird's-eye view of the fleet of aircraft—two thousand of them, the pilot told him—that the Allies had amassed. "They were ready to pound Japan. Tokyo would have been completely flattened. Osaka would have been completely flattened." The other big cities, too.

Not everyone shares that view, but then not everyone has Hoenson's perspective. Like the astronauts who walked on the moon, his is an exclusive club. Perhaps one of the reasons he stayed silent for all these years is that none of the rest of us could truly relate to what he lived through.

bonsai bob

NOT EVERYONE WHO survived capture in the Dutch East Indies recovered like Rudi Hoenson.

Long before the body of Bob Deryk—Bonsai Bob—was found near his Eden by the Sooke Potholes, it was obvious he was beset by demons.

A childhood in a Japanese concentration camp had left him with a lifelong fear of being locked up again. The experience shaped his life and brought him to the unfenced, uncrowded refuge he carved out of the forest. After he was found dead, apparently by his own hand, you wondered if he just couldn't stand the idea of going to prison, of losing his wilderness home.

His body was found in February 2013 just a stone's throw from his cabin, less than two weeks after it was learned he had, at age seventy-four, been charged with sexually assaulting two minors. News of his arrest bewildered some of his friends and outraged others. Long after his death, many would not, could not believe the charges had merit. In truth, without knowing more about the case—privacy rules prevented police from saying much—it was hard to either defend or condemn him.

What is known is that his story had a sad start and a sad end. He told me the tale one day in 2006, surrounded by the hundreds of bonsai trees that gave him his nickname.

I found him clad in purple swim trunks and ball cap, plunked on the cabin's veranda, gluing dime-sized rocks together—part of a bonsai display he had been asked to mount at the Sooke Region Museum. He said he wasn't quite sure why he had agreed to do so. After all, he was a private, even reclusive, man (though not a hermit), craving neither fame nor attention. "That's why I live in a leave-me-alone cabin," he said.

He had a quiet manner, a wry wit. A stone's toss below, the Sooke River danced over the rocks. It would have been an idyllic scene, this splendid isolation, if you didn't know his history.

Deryk was only three years old when the Japanese invaded the country now known as Indonesia in 1942. They just appeared one day, rumbling down the road, hustling the bewildered Dutch colonials out of their homes and into army trucks. All males over the age of fourteen were shipped to one camp, the women and children to another. Deryk, his older brother, and his mother ended up in Tjideng, a fenced-off part of Jakarta, six families jammed into a house. A camp that began with two hundred people swelled toward twenty thousand.

"The food was totally inadequate," Deryk said. Protein was non-existent. Mostly they ate mung beans. There was no medicine to counter the rampant beriberi, dysentery, and other diseases. Three-quarters of the prisoners perished, he said. "My mum said six more months and we would have died."

The brutality of the guards was seared into his memory. "They did horrible things. The women were beaten left and right." Every day at noon, the prisoners—the elderly, the sick, everyone—were herded into the square to stand in the burning white heat and bow before the commandant (who was later executed as a war criminal). Sometimes the guards would keep the women and children standing there all night, just because they could. Sometimes a woman would be forced to bunny-hop along the line of prisoners, and, prodded by rifle butts, keep on bunny-hopping until she dropped from exhaustion. Then the guards would beat the guts out of her.

Deryk—three, four, five, six years old—lived all this. It left him, and the other survivors, scarred. "We're known as the Forgotten Ones," he said. "We're all totally screwed up."

More than sixty years later, the war's effects remained profound. "We all live with a little suitcase in a corner of the room," he said. His was packed with the essentials of life— a toothbrush, coffee, that sort of thing. "I'm always looking down the road, wondering: 'Are they coming to get me today?'" It doesn't take much to link that lost childhood in a barbed-wire hell to an adulthood spent under the radar, off in the woods.

Somehow, he, his brother, and his mother survived the war and were reunited with Deryk's father. "I didn't even know what a dad was. I asked my mum, 'Is that man coming again tomorrow?'"

They moved to Holland, but Deryk didn't like it. Too cold, too crowded. In 1957, when Deryk was eighteen, Canada beckoned. He got a job at the veterinary college in Guelph.

Deryk eventually moved to Victoria and was the gardener at Fable Cottage before it was barged off to Denman Island in 1993. He was living in a Cordova Bay garage in 1994 when he hooked up with Albert Yuen, owner of the five-kilometre-long Deertrail property that hugged the Sooke River and its famous potholes. Yuen wanted Deryk to grow food for the lodge Yuen wanted to open there.

So Deryk was installed in a dilapidated little cabin high up on the property. Don't fix the place up, Deryk was told, you'll only be in it for six months or so. He was there almost twenty years.

By the time I met him, Deryk had made the cabin homey, put in doors and windows, made cedar shakes. He had an outhouse, a garden shed, a wood-heated sauna. No electricity, no running water except that drawn from the Sooke River. The burbling river, mingled with the music of the wind chimes and the occasional birdsong, was all he heard. "I still think it's the best place in the world."

Of course, the Deertrail dream never came true (though for years the massive stone chimneys and open timbers of a partially built structure showed how close it got). After a court ordered the sale of the property in 2003 and it was purchased as parkland, Deryk remained as a resident caretaker, albeit one who said he wasn't sure how long he would remain, as more and more people came stumbling across his cabin. After the parks department improved access to the potholes, even women in high heels trod trails once limited to hiking boots.

In 2006 he said that if some outfit came up with a proposal where he could resettle with his bonsai collection, displaying and nurturing it in a proper greenhouse, he would probably go for the deal. Give him $75,000 for the trees and he would be on the first plane for Bali; he could still smell the vegetation, taste the fresh mangoes.

It was hard to imagine him parting with the bonsai trees, though. They were, he admitted, "a total obsession." It was an infatuation that began in 1965 with a single jade tree that he brought inside to protect from the Ontario winter. Perched atop his television, it cast a shadow resembling a bonsai—and triggered something inside Deryk.

Forty years later, he figured he had grown a thousand bonsais—the word means "potted tree"—since then. They took on personalities, character slowly shaped into trees that could be hundreds of years old. Deryk would grow them from oak, white pine, larch, cedar—anything but arbutus (too hard and messy) or banana (leaves are too big). "To me, it's totally irresistible," he said. "It's living art."

He had four hundred bonsai trees in Ontario and brought one hundred to Fable Cottage. By the time he died, the Japanese-style gate he installed at the edge of the property gave way to somewhere between seven hundred and a thousand carefully tended trees. Beyond them, at the end of the path, stood his shingled cottage, its orange trim and orange flag an apparent nod to Deryk's Dutch roots.

The tranquillity was deceiving, though. His body was found in an implement shed not far away, ending the sad story of Bonsai Bob.

the veterans

EARL CLARK STILL flashes back to D-Day.

"Every once in a while you wake up in the night and, boom, you're right there," the ninety-seven-year-old says, gripping the arms of his wheelchair.

He can hear the mortar rounds raining down, see the machine-gun rounds slapping the water like heavy hail as the Canadian Scottish Regiment—all those Victoria boys, Nanaimo boys, Comox Valley boys—poured onto Juno Beach.

"As soon as the landing barges hit the beach, we had to race like crazy, because if you stayed on the beach for one second, you were going to get mowed down."

Up the slope they scrambled, weighed down with gear— rifle, pack, a short-handled shovel.

It wasn't any safer when they reached the top. "That's where Jerry had his fortifications. He poured the lead at us."

The Canadians had to keep their legs moving if they wanted to stay alive. "You'd go a few feet, hit the ground, roll over, and do that again." Stay in one spot, the machine guns would zero in. "You just kept going."

It was awful. "There were dead and dying all over the place." Canadians. Germans and their allies. They all fell.

"It was just a sea of dead and dying. You never forget it."

There is no bravado to Earl Clark's story, no flag-waving. The opposite, in fact. He reddens and trembles a bit, has to pause while reliving the day. Behind him in their room at Saanich's Veterans Lodge at Broadmead, his wife, Margaret, her posture perfect, listens to her husband's story in silence.

THAT WAS IN 2014, exactly seventy years after D-Day and two before Earl Clark died.

This wasn't John Wayne in *The Longest Day* or Tom Hanks in *Saving Private Ryan*. Clark was a salt-of-the-earth guy from Vancouver Island, not an actor, and what is Hollywood—or history—to the rest of us was real life to him.

Real life to a lot of other Islanders, too. Vancouver Island sacrificed disproportionately on June 6, 1944. The soldiers of the first battalion of the Victoria-based Canadian Scottish Regiment were among the first ashore when fourteen thousand Canadians landed in Normandy that day. Other Islanders piloted landing craft through the mine-strewn surf or parachuted into the blackness of the pre-invasion night.

It has been a source of national pride ever since, Canada being assigned one of the five invasion beaches (Sword and Gold went to the British, Omaha and Utah to the US) for one of the most significant battles in history.

The Royal Canadian Navy was there, too, ten thousand sailors in 109 ships bombarding the French coastline and carrying troops and supplies through the heavily mined waters. The Royal Canadian Air Force also had a hand in Operation Overlord, the official name of the invasion of western Europe.

Over the years, I got to write about a lot of D-Day vets, few of whom remain today. Chester Stefanek was on Juno Beach in

1944, drove a transport vehicle while under fire. Bill Fisher's role in the invasion involved jumping out of a plane. Peter Ramsay led a company of the Canadian Scottish in the first wave to hit his section of French soil. Bob Parlow was offshore aboard HMCS *St. Laurent*, which was firing at German positions. Frank Poole's D-Day mission was to lead enemy fighters away from the Allied bombers. He was eventually shot down over Germany and ended up in a prisoner of war camp.

CLARK WAS A logger before the war, part of a hard-working pioneer family in Shirley, past Sooke, where he grew up with eight brothers and a sister. He was a logger during the war, too, serving in the Canadian Forestry Corps in northern Scotland. That's where he met Margaret, she of the lovely brogue, at a dance. "At least I didn't step on her toes," he said. They were married for seventy-four years.

Clark was shifted to the Canadian Scottish just before D-Day. A Polish ship ferried his company across the English Channel. They scrambled down netting hanging from its hull to get to the landing craft that ran them to Juno Beach. He recalled that a Major English was in charge. He remembered another officer, too. "His tank got hit and he lost both his legs."

By the end of the day, the regiment was ten kilometres inland, farther than anyone else.

The Canadian Scottish experience was well-documented in *Ready for the Fray*, the regimental history written by Reg Roy in 1957. The infantry unit lost eighty-seven soldiers on D-Day. More than two hundred men, almost a third of the battalion's pre-invasion strength, had become casualties by the fourth day of fighting. The battle for the town of Putot-en-Bessin alone saw forty-five Canadian Scottish killed and another eighty wounded. (The Royal Winnipeg Rifles suffered there, too, including a couple of dozen men who were flat-out murdered by SS troops after being taken prisoner.)

On D-Day itself, some of the Canadian Scottish were ferried across the English Channel aboard the *Prince Henry*, which in peacetime served the BC coast as a Canadian National steamship. That resulted in some halfway-around-the-world reunions: as Lieutenant Stew Ross of the CanScots marched up the gangplank in England, he dropped the eighty pounds of gear on his back and embraced twenty-three-year-old Lieutenant Jack Davie, the leader of the ship's flotilla of landing craft. "Then Ross took Davie to a shipboard reunion with Maj. Dick Lendrum, who used to teach them both in the high school at Duncan, BC," reported a newspaperman aboard the *Prince Henry*.

Ross did not survive the war, but Davie and Lendrum did—and remained friends. "After the war I used to say to Dick that putting him on the beach in Normandy was my revenge for him trying to teach me Latin," Davie told me one day in 2001.

That was in Davie's Maple Bay home at a reunion with six others who had lived through that day: Jimmy Mason of the *Prince Henry*'s crew and five—Billy Lindsay, Herb Millar, Frank Maxwell, Doug Townson, and Dave Paterson (the father of journalist Jody Paterson)—who had ferried the soldiers ashore aboard the ship's landing craft. The boats were basically wooden-bottomed, armour-sided barges designed to carry about thirty soldiers and a crew of four.

It was about ten kilometres from the *Prince Henry* to the Normandy beach, but things didn't start getting hairy until the landing craft tried to wriggle through the obstacles—heavy steel tripods, many of them wired with Teller mines and percussion-tipped artillery shells—that the Germans had strewn thickly through the beach and shallows.

Mortar bombs began falling among them. One exploded as coxswain Townson was weaving his boat through the obstacles. It left him with a piece of shrapnel that remained in his head for the rest of his life. ("It wasn't much," he shrugged in 2001. "It just knocked me out, is all.")

Townson recovered and kept pushing for the beach. His craft unloaded the troops, but a line fouled on something and the boat drifted sideways until it hit a mine. It was the other guys who related how Townson and crew pulled his badly wounded stoker out of the belly of the vessel, how they put out the fire before the flames reached the fuel tanks.

Things went a bit better in Davie's craft. They gave their Canadian Scottish a dry landing and were about to pull out when they saw a wounded corporal from the Royal Winnipeg Rifles calling for help. Davie half-carried him back to the landing craft, kicking stray wires out of their feet on the way. "Little did I know that these were rusted trip wires designed to detonate the bombs between the beach obstacles," related Davie. "We put this fellow on a stretcher, gave him a shot of morphine, and just as we backed off the beach a wave pushed us onto a beach obstacle, which holed us."

Two other landing craft, including Paterson's, tied up to Davie's and got it safely back to the *Prince Henry*. ("The crew bailed furiously because they didn't think they could make it," wrote a reporter who interviewed Davie after he returned to the ship.)

Their D-Day experience could have been worse, said Paterson. "It wasn't as bad as we expected." There was lots of shrapnel flying around, but "those obstacles took your mind off the rest of the stuff."

Roy's history offered another perspective. While only one of the *Prince Henry*'s eight landing craft was lost, all eight belonging to another ship, the *Prince David*, were destroyed. Heavy seas swamped tank landing craft several kilometres from shore. Concentrated mortar fire from the shore knocked out many tanks before the landing craft even reached the beach. Many soldiers (including those who had disembarked from the *Prince Henry*, whose crew had provided the Canadian Scottish with a much-appreciated lunch of two boiled eggs and a cheese sandwich to add to their rations) became seasick.

On shore, the fighting was relatively light in places, furious in others. An Indigenous soldier, Private B.M. Francis, killed two or three snipers, including one he shot from the hip without aiming, from a distance of fifty metres, before himself being killed, Roy wrote. Ordered to take out a dangerous German gun emplacement, Lieutenant Bernie Clarke replied with the now-legendary "Who? *Me*?" before doing the job. Hardest hit of all was a platoon led by Lieutenant Roger Schjelderup, a young officer from Courtenay.

I found out about Schjelderup by accident one day in 2000 while leafing through a file of old Second World War photos gathering dust in the *Times Colonist* library. One of the fading black-and-whites, an army public relations picture, showed a pair of pyjama-clad D-Day casualties perched on a British hospital bed, cigarettes in hands, playing cards. It was the kind of frozen-in-time image that makes you wonder what happened to its subjects, which is why I looked them up.

One of the card players was Schjelderup, who had proven himself remarkable even before joining the army. In 1937, at age fifteen, he climbed Vancouver Island's highest mountain, the 2,200-metre Golden Hinde, just after a team of surveyors made the first recorded ascent of the peak. He went on to become one of the most highly decorated Canadians of the Second World War.

He was among the first ashore on D-Day. ("He said 'Our footprints were the first in the sand,'" his widow, Ida Schjelderup, told me a few years ago.) By nightfall no platoon had been hit harder than Schjelderup's, wrote Roy. "He had come ashore with 45 men under his command. At the end of the day when he, himself, was ordered back to have his wounds dressed, there were only 19 men left."

Schjelderup's actions earned him the Military Cross. By October he was back in action on the Holland-Belgium border, where he led a company that stubbornly held off a massive counterattack long enough for other troops to get in position to prevent the Germans from recrossing the Leopold Canal. But Schjelderup, wounded by a grenade and with his headquarters on fire, was captured. He wasn't a prisoner long. Two weeks later, using a penknife that a Sergeant Gri had managed to hide, the Canadians cut their way out of the box-car in which they were held. A farmer hooked them up with the Dutch Resistance, whom the Canadians joined in raiding German targets.

It took Schjelderup several weeks to recover from his wounds and pneumonia, but in late December he was in a small group that set out for Allied lines. It was a harrowing journey: shot at by the enemy, slowed by snow, crossing canals covered by ice not quite thick enough to bear a man. "A number of times the group stumbled over trip wires leading to mines and booby traps which, with their mechanism frozen solid, did not go off," wrote Roy.

Finally, on January 5, 1945, the ragged band was taken in by the forward troops of a British unit, who fed them tea laced with rum.

Schjelderup was awarded the Distinguished Service Order (a rare honour for a junior officer) for the Leopold Canal and a bar on his Military Cross for his actions later.

That's a very stripped-down version of a dramatic story, the kind of tale that would have been made into a Hollywood movie were Schjelderup from another country. Instead, few of us even know his name. After Schjelderup's death in 1974, it was left to his childhood friend and fellow outdoor enthusiast Ruth Masters—a much-respected Vancouver Island environmentalist—to drive the campaign to have a Strathcona Park lake near the Golden Hinde named in his memory. Even then, the parks branch balked at allowing a memorial cairn beside Schjelderup Lake. Magically, a plaque appeared there in 2002. Family members gave it a proper blessing: "We poured half a bottle of Johnnie Walker into the lake," Schjelderup's son Eric later said. Every year, one or more family members make the arduous, three-day hike in to pay their respects.

While Schjelderup had died by the time I learned of his story, the other soldier in that army public relations photo was very much alive. Ken Byron relayed his story in person when photographer Debra Brash and I tracked him down to the family farm on Salt Spring Island, where he had been born and raised.

On the day we met, he was supposed to be getting an MRI, but Victoria General Hospital sent him home after learning about the shrapnel in his head. They feared it would heat up and throw off the test.

The shrapnel had been there since D-Day, when he landed as a twenty-three-year-old platoon sergeant. He hadn't even trod on French soil before finding himself in charge; his officer, Lieutenant Hector Russell, was badly wounded when a bomb hit their landing craft just as its ramp dropped on the shore at Vaux.

"I was platoon commander as soon as I hit the beach," Byron said.

He didn't have to wait long for his own wound. "Mortar bombs started to drop. I dove into a tank trap. My mortar man dropped right in front of me, dead. He got a piece of shrapnel in his temple. I got a piece in my cheek, cut the artery."

A doctor patched up Byron to the point where, though coated in a mixture of sand and blood, he was able to lead the platoon inland. "I stayed in the battle for the rest of the day."

They shipped him back to England. No sooner had he been tucked into bed in Basingstoke Hospital than the buzz bombs began falling, with their awful moan. "When they landed, you were happy because you knew they hadn't hit you."

He was shifted to Ascot with the rest of the Canadian Scottish wounded, including Schjelderup. It was there that a photographer posed the pair for the photo.

He made his way back to Normandy in mid-July 1944, taking command of his old platoon. The Canadian Scottish saw plenty of action, but what really remained etched in his memory was the road to Falaise in mid-August: death, destruction, flies, heat, shattered carts, burning tanks, "the thick, grey dust about a foot and a half deep." Allied aircraft had pounded the Germans caught on the road, and bulldozers had then plowed through the carnage, making a path for the advancing Canadians. "Dead men, horses, livestock in nearby fields, all rotting," recalled Byron. "The smell is still with me."

The end of August found Byron trying to fight his platoon out of the French town of Tourville amid heavy artillery fire. "All of a sudden something caught me and spun me around to the ground." Shrapnel had ripped into his arm and side. "The flesh had been torn off my hipbone."

As he waited to be evacuated, a shell slammed into the bare hillside where he lay and tumbled end over end without exploding. "If that thing had gone off, I wouldn't be here to tell you the story."

He recovered to fight on until VE Day, served in Korea, and stayed in the army until 1976, when he retired to Salt Spring Island. Never married, he lived and farmed alone despite a long-running series of cancers he traced to 1966, when the American military—with Ottawa's blessing—sprayed New Brunswick's CFB Gagetown with Agent Orange, infamous as a Vietnam War defoliant. When he died in 2014, he went out the way he wanted: in his own bed on the Salt Spring farm where he stubbornly lived alone. He was ninety-three. Tough old guy.

So was his one-year-younger brother, Terry, who lived alone on his own farm just down the road, raising ponies and beef cattle (he had chickens until his dog died, after which the raccoons came in and wiped them all out). Terry was another of the big contingent of Salt Spring teens who volunteered to go overseas in 1939. "When the war broke out, all us guys who had been in the militia joined up," he said.

Like his big brother, Terry was a sergeant who was wounded in battle. In his case it was in Belgium on October 13, 1944: "I was leading the platoon on the Leopold Canal. Most of us got across. It was midnight, eh? When I thought it was appropriate, I stood up and a goddamned German grenade landed right in front of me."

He didn't take the full blast, just enough to rip apart his left knee. Trapped between the Germans and the canal, he crawled along until he found himself looking down a couple of gun barrels. "'Who are you?' they asked. I said, 'Canadian Scottish.'" They were Royal Winnipeg Rifles, who got him to a stretcher-boat.

When I met Terry in 2013, he didn't want to dwell on the bad bits. "It was a tough go, but you try to forget the tough stuff and remember the funny things, the good people you meet."

Some stories still cracked him up, like the time the Canadian Scottish's Wing Hay, a noted boxer from Port Alberni, saw some chickens running loose. Hay figured that where there were hens, there would be fresh eggs to eat, so he went looking in a barn. Alas, instead of eggs he found a dozen or so German soldiers. "All these buggers stood up and put their hands up." The single-handed capture made headlines on both sides of the Atlantic.

Then there was May 8, 1945. His wounds healed, Terry was in Aldershot, England, waiting to be posted back to the front, when word came down that Germany had surrendered. The sergeants' mess went dry pretty quickly after that. "What they didn't drink, they threw at each other." So Terry sought out Big Nan, a strapping Scottish woman with access to the officers' mess. "She said, 'I pilfered this bottle of whisky from the officers' supply, so you, me, and these two girls are going to have a snort.'" With that, they drained the bottle.

That sort of tale was common among the veterans when you tried to pry war stories out of them. They didn't want to talk about the bad days. When I met the landing-craft veterans at their D-Day reunion at Davie's house, getting them to talk about the invasion was like trying to teach a cat to fetch.

Oh, they would talk, all right. In fact, the longer they talked, the younger they got. It was just that not much of the conversation was about the day they filled their landing craft with soldiers and drove them onto Juno Beach.

They talked about Greenberg, the Jewish crewmate who arrived at their ship wearing a German uniform.

They talked about the time—it was after the North Africa and Sicily landings—when they got posted to Victoria to join the *Prince Henry*. There was a bit of a party at Yates and Douglas that ended up with a few of the boys trading clothes with some girls and trading punches with some guys. "Where are your uniforms?" asked the judge when they appeared in court. They pointed to the girls.

Then there was the time in Southampton, England, when they decided an American officer they had been hosting was too drunk to drive. They sent him off with some gin, telling him he could collect his vehicle in the morning—then hoisted it on deck before steaming off to war. "We decided we could do with a jeep on the ship," reasoned Davie.

"We had the old paintbrush out as soon as we got it on board, too," added Jimmy Mason.

It turned out to be quite a useful automobile in their journeys, at least until they found out the Americans were looking for it, at which point they traded it to some Eighth Army fellows in Alexandria, Egypt, for a brand new one. That second jeep also served them well, at least until the car chase with the London cops, after which it was decided to park it in the Thames beside the East India Docks.

Funny story, but most of what I learned about their actual D-Day experience came from Davie's written account. None of the old boys at Davie's house wanted to talk about it. Every one of them is gone now, their memories gone with them.

That's how it is with so many of the Second World War veterans I wrote about over the years. I'm glad I got to preserve snippets of their stories.

SIDNEY'S LYNN HENSHAW was just sixteen years and one month old when he and the rest of the South Saskatchewan Regiment stormed the beach at Dieppe. He didn't expect to make it out. "I was ready for a bullet to hit me."

When, a year later, the Canadian Army weeded out underage soldiers, Henshaw's immediate response was to join the merchant marine. That's when he got the tattoos on his forearms.

LANGFORD'S JIM VINCENT got tattoos, too—a cowboy on one arm, an Indian on the other—but for his own reasons. They were the best way of telling the German guards that he was a Canadian, not an "Englander" like the others in his POW camp.

Vincent endured three escapes, three captures, and three Christmases in a German salt mine. That was after he was captured at Puys, during the Dieppe raid of 1942. A private in the Royal Regiment of Canada, he was in the second wave of assault craft, watching as the first wave landed. "We heard a lot of firing. Then it went dead silent. We couldn't figure out why." The answer was horrible: the first wave was wiped out, slaughtered as soon as the doors on the landing craft dropped.

Then it was Vincent's turn. Laden with smoke bombs and high explosives for his two-inch mortar, he plunged into the water—and was immediately blown to the shore's edge by an explosion. "I was just lifted off my feet into the water."

Vincent had caught a load of shrapnel in the back. It cut the strap of his haversack; two inches over and it would have set off his mortar bombs. "I still wonder how come I got out of there. Why me?"

He almost didn't get out. He lay senseless at the water's edge as machine-gunfire rained down. After a while, with the tide moving in, he groggily moved his head, which caught the eye of a comrade. "Somebody yelled, 'Vincent's still there,'" and a brave soul pulled himself away from the base of the seawall and dragged Vincent to relative safety. It took him twenty-five years to find out who rescued him; the man died a month before Vincent discovered his saviour's name.

EARL TAYLOR WAS an RCAF air gunner when his Lancaster bomber was hit during a raid over Berlin on March 29, 1943. With three of the four engines in flames, the crew bailed out into the 1 AM blackness.

Taylor's parachute snagged in a tree. Not knowing how far above the ground he was, he stayed suspended until the light of dawn. Turned out he wasn't that high up.

His freedom was short-lived. The Lancaster's entire crew was taken prisoner, and not all survived the war. The skipper, Denys Street, was one of those shot in the back after being recaptured following the Great Escape.

Taylor himself ended up in a succession of POW camps in what are now Poland and Lithuania. Sometimes the captives were treated decently, sometimes not. Once, German guards with snarling Alsatians and Dobermans ran the prisoners— some in handcuffs, all burdened with packs—three kilometres from a train station to a new camp, beating and bayonetting those who fell back. The airmen were beaten again while running a gauntlet into the camp.

In February 1945, with the Russians advancing from the east, the prisoners began a month-long march west in sub-zero temperatures. They were sick, starving. "We used to pick frozen vegetables out of the ground when we had the chance." Those who couldn't stagger on simply disappeared.

Taylor kept hope—"It was always there, that you hoped to come home one day"—until he was finally liberated by Russian soldiers.

And then he came back and, like close to a million other Canadians, quietly picked up the pieces. Got married, had kids, opened Taylor's Pharmacy in Cordova Bay. His daughters said he never talked about the war much.

"I don't dwell on it," he said in 2011, sitting in a Broadmead Lodge room decorated with family photos and cycling trophies. "It's not worthwhile. There are other things to do."

CROFTON'S DENIS HIGGINS was but fourteen years old when he signed on as a cabin boy in Britain's merchant marine in 1941. The death of his brother, a submariner killed off Italy in 1940, might have had something to do with his decision to enlist so young.

He was still fourteen when he was sunk for the first time. It was at night, in the South Atlantic en route to Sierra Leone, when the torpedoes struck. He was eleven days in a lifeboat before they washed up in the Canary Islands. While adrift, two of the men in the lifeboat drank seawater, went crazy, and leapt into the ocean, lost forever.

Later, Higgins was on a convoy to the Soviet Union—the dreaded Murmansk run—when his ship, laden with tanks, crated Spitfires, ammunition, and other war supplies, was discovered and attacked by two dive-bombers. One bomb slammed into the vessel amidships—and kept on going, right through the other side, exploding in the water. The damaged ship limped into Murmansk, where it was again attacked from the air and sank right beside the wharf. "I had my sixteenth birthday in Murmansk."

He was in the Bay of Biscay in 1943 when sunk for the third time, his ship struck by a flying bomb. He went over the side with his buddy Chris. Rescuers found Higgins, who regained his senses the next day. They never found Chris.

It always rankled that the merchant seamen were ignored by British officialdom after the war. "They didn't regard us as members of the armed forces."

ALF TRUEMAN SERVED in Britain's Eighth Army—the famed Desert Rats—while Henry Demski was in Germany's Afrika Korps when the tide of the war turned at Alamein, Egypt, in 1942.

Both came close to death in that campaign. One soldier was killed, another wounded, when Trueman's Bren gun carrier hit a landmine. A mine blew a wheel off Demski's truck, too. Years after the war, Demski's wife was still picking shrapnel out of his legs.

As the fighting wound down in North Africa, so did the will to kill, Demski said. "The last week, nobody likes to shoot anymore. Nobody likes to die anymore." Twice, when on reconnaissance in the desert, Demski was shooed back to his own lines by Allied soldiers. The sides were close enough to see the glow of the other's pre-dawn cigarettes but refrained from firing. Once, when the melody of "Lili Marlene" drifted over from the British lines, the Germans sang along.

On July 31, 2013, Demski and Trueman celebrated their birthdays together at The Glenshiel seniors' home in Victoria, where they lived and were best of friends.

"If Rommel could see us now," Trueman said, nudging Demski.

"My brother," replied Demski, patting Trueman on the hand.

IT'S NOT UNCOMMON for soldiers to desert in wartime, but Oak Bay's Noel (Bach) Parker-Jervis might have been the only one to run toward the action.

He had hoped to go overseas when he signed up at age eighteen in 1939, but his eyesight was so bad that he was posted first to a two-gun artillery unit at Point Grey, staving off the less-than-likely Nazi invasion of the University of British Columbia, then to tiny Yorke Island off Vancouver Island, staving off an attack by lord knows whom.

Repeatedly frustrated in his attempts to go overseas, he took matters into his own hands. He took a train to Halifax and worked on a cargo ship to England, where he turned himself in. The army went easy on him, and he ended up getting what he wanted, going into action in Italy in an anti-tank tank. The open-turreted armoured vehicle carried a rear-mounted .50 calibre machine gun whose muzzle flash would come right down on Parker-Jervis's head, leaving him with the "gunner's deafness" that still afflicted him in his nineties.

ATHOLL SUTHERLAND BROWN'S most nerve-racking mission, scarier even than the time he was wounded, came while attacking a complex of Japanese airfields in central Burma. He was flying a two-man Beaufighter, had just shot up four trucks and watched them explode, when his ammunition ran out during another run. Go south a bit before turning, his navigator said, but Sutherland Brown didn't listen, banked for home. Bad idea.

"The flak started coming up from all over the place." The aircraft was hit, hydraulic fluid pouring out of the port side. Sutherland Brown climbed to three thousand feet, drew more big puffs of exploding anti-aircraft fire, dived for the deck again. A shell blasted the radio apart, right in the navigator's face.

A sitting duck, riddled with thirty-nine holes, the Beaufighter limped to safety, two and a half hours away. No flaps. Couldn't get the landing gear down. "I had to crash-land at the base when I got there."

WITH THE SHIP ablaze, the crew of HMCS *Athabaskan* tried to lower the lifeboats. No good. The mechanism jammed.

So Doug Laurie waited until the destroyer began to drop at the stern and roll on its starboard side before he slid down the hull of the doomed vessel and into the inky blackness of the English Channel. Then, afraid of being snared by dangling wires, he swam away as fast as he could.

He could see the illumination of little battery-powered lights that some of the sailors wore on their heads, but that was all—save for the dark mass of the *Athabaskan* rising straight in the air, then straight under the surface. Floating in the blackness, he talked to another crew member for a bit, but then that man went silent, didn't make it.

Laurie tried to swim to *Athabaskan's* sister ship, HMCS *Haida*, actually getting within ten metres. "They threw me a life ring, but I never caught it—and they had to go," he said. The *Haida* rescued more than forty survivors before bolting to safety, but left twice that many in the water. Coated in oil, an exhausted Laurie drifted off, floating for four hours before he and more than eighty other Canadians were picked up by German vessels.

They were the lucky ones. The April 29, 1944, sinking of the *Athabaskan* was one of the worst losses in Canadian naval history. A total of 128 sailors died that night, including the ship's commanding officer, Lieutenant Commander John Stubbs, whose name lives on in a Victoria-area elementary school.

Laurie's German rescuers cut off his oil-soaked clothes with a big knife. "I was left naked on the quarterdeck." Then it was off to spend the last year of the war in a camp between Bremen and Hanover.

Sixty-seven years later, when I met him in a Victoria hospital where he was recovering from surgery, Laurie could still remember questioning his German interrogator. "I said, 'What's going to happen to me?' He said, 'We're going to put you in cells for the rest of your life.'"

Laurie lost twenty pounds in that camp, living on turnips and Red Cross parcels from home. "The Germans got there first. They took whatever they wanted out of the parcels. We lived on what was left."

The other prisoners told him he wouldn't be so hungry if he started smoking, so he did, thanks to the cigarettes in those same parcels.

Those smokes had other uses, too. "Cigarettes were money," he told his family. "You bartered with the Germans. They'd sell their soul for cigarettes." A British prisoner even traded for a radio, a clandestine way to track the progress of the war.

As the Allies approached, the guards were shedding their uniforms, trying to pass themselves off as civilians. The British soldiers who liberated the camp asked which guards were the worst. The "mean" ones were marched outside the wire. The prisoners heard shots.

Back home, Laurie's new Scottish war bride, Ingar, had only been in Canada six weeks when she learned the *Athabaskan* had been sunk. "I remember getting the telegram. I was up in Port Alberni, visiting friends."

It wasn't until August that she learned her husband's fate, word coming via a postcard from Laurie himself, sent from the POW camp. "I knew his handwriting. It just said, 'I am well.' Everything else was scored out. I knew then that he was alive."

She told me this while standing in his hospital room, watching over her husband of sixty-eight years, one of the lucky ones who came home.

IN THE EVENINGS, Mac Colquhoun would stroll the grounds of the prisoner-of-war camp with bags of dirt hidden inside his clothing.

Pull a string—sitting in his room in the Lodge at Broadmead, the ninety-eight-year-old reached in his pockets to show how it was done—and the sandy soil would fall out of his pant legs.

That's how the Allied prisoners got rid of the dirt from their escape tunnel. Maybe you saw that scene depicted in classic Second World War movies, such as *The Wooden Horse* and *The Great Escape*, but Colquhoun actually lived it.

Colquhoun was a Saskatchewan farm boy whose Royal Canadian Air Force bomber was crippled by heavy flak west of Dusseldorf, Germany, one January night in 1943. Flight Lieutenant Colquhoun, the navigator, parachuted into a farmer's field. Another man landed safely, too, though a third died in the attempt. The other four crew members and the plane itself were never accounted for.

Colquhoun ended up in a Luftwaffe-run POW camp near the town of Sagan, now part of Poland. It's where both the events shown in *The Wooden Horse* and *The Great Escape* took place. He was directly involved in the former, a clever escapade in which prisoners used the plywood from Red Cross crates to build a gymnastics horse, which, every day, they would carry to the same spot in the prison yard—right over the hidden entrance to a tunnel. Inside the hollow exercise apparatus were hidden one or two prisoners who would do the digging, carefully covering the tunnel entrance with wood and topsoil before being carried back inside with that day's excavated dirt.

"My department was looking after hiding the dirt that came out," Colquhoun says. "I hauled a lot of dirt."

It was tricky, though.

The yellow sand from the tunnel stood out from the surface soil. "As soon as that showed up, they knew we were digging."

So some of the sand was buried under the camp's many vegetable gardens. Some was stored in a roof. Some was poured down holes cut in a theatre stage. Much was dispersed through the down-the-leg method described earlier. The bags that held the sand were about four feet long, sewn from old pant legs and hooked to the wearer's suspenders. As Colquhoun and others dribbled the sand out, other prisoners would scuff it into the dirt. "We made sure everybody in the camp was out walking when we had this sand to spread."

In October 1943, three prisoners escaped.

"The people who were selected spoke German, knew the country, and had a decent chance of getting home." Indeed, all three made it to Britain safely.

The same couldn't be said of the Great Escape, hatched just across the wire in a neighbouring compound within the Sagan camp. "We knew what was going on, but it was across the fence from us."

Of the seventy-six who escaped, seventy-three were recaptured, and fifty of those—including six Canadians—were executed. Colquhoun heard that Adolf Hitler himself decided which of the prisoners would be killed. "They were all shot. All they did was escape. There's no law against that, but that was Hitler's cure."

As for the 1963 *Great Escape* movie, it was largely accurate, though there were no Americans among the escapees and, no, nobody jumped the barbed wire on a motorcycle, Colquhoun said. "Steve McQueen had to have a role that made him do something that benefited his career in the movies."

On January 27, 1945, exactly two years after Colquhoun was shot down, and with Russian soldiers streaming past, the Sagan prisoners were ordered west to a German camp near Denmark. It was a brutal journey, thirty below zero, and the POWs had no winter wear. "It was desperately cold, nowhere to go at night, just about the worst you can think of." The other surviving member of Colquhoun's bomber crew was among those who froze to death. "I thought I was lucky that I had walked to school on the Prairies and knew what cold was."

In May, as Germany descended into end-of-the-war chaos, the prison guards disappeared. Rather than wait for liberators to arrive, Colquhoun and four others took matters into their own hands, commandeering a car that they drove two hundred kilometres to an airport that they knew was being used by the Allies. They made it to London just in time to get in on the wild VE Day celebrations in Piccadilly Circus.

On March 1, 2018, Mac Colquhoun turned 101.

SOME NIGHTS, DIEPPE comes back to Ken Curry as though it were yesterday.

It was a slaughter as soon as the ramps dropped, the water red with the blood of dead and dying Canadians. The sounds were terrible, the screaming of the wounded punctuated by the shells raining down from clifftop artillery, the bombs falling from German planes.

The Bren gun carrier that Curry followed out of his landing craft was blown from the water. The twenty-year-old bandaged the knee of his wounded sergeant, but the man was later killed by a bullet to his head. Of the seven men who wrestled Curry's mortar and ammunition ashore, four were cut down.

Machine guns chewed into the Canadians from the windows of beachfront hotels. No aiming—the Germans just had to pull the trigger. Setting up the mortar on a rocky shore, Curry fought back. "I fired thirty-two bombs into them, but I don't think it did any good," the Sidney man said.

But then, not much good came out of the Dieppe raid of August 19, 1942.

It was Canada's costliest day of the Second World War. Of the 5,000 Canadians—along with 1,100 British and 50 Americans—who landed at the French coastal town, more than 900 were killed and 2,400 wounded. Close to 2,000 were captured.

"Dieppe was one big fiasco," Curry said. The soldiers were told the raid would be easy, that they would face only a single beat-up battalion recuperating from the Russian front. "They didn't mention the SS regiments and the tank regiments that were waiting for us." A skirmish with a German convoy took away the element of surprise, too.

He remembers the six hours he spent pinned on that beach, the incessant machine-gun chatter punctuated by bombs falling from German planes. Next to him, a tank that had lost a track on the rocks fired off round after deafening round. Curry couldn't figure out what the hell the tank was shooting at. "All the time that I'm lying there, he's firing that gun." (Years later, Curry met the gunner. "I was just trying to get rid of the shells," the man told him. "I didn't want to get blown up if we got hit." Curry was later awarded a pension for his partial loss of hearing.)

Finally, the navy put down a smokescreen and the evacuation began. Curry used four captured Germans to bundle two wounded men, one a friend, the other a major, onto a boat. The coxswain wouldn't let anyone but the wounded aboard, though, so Curry took his four Germans and tried another vessel, only to end up back in the water after it took three direct hits and started to sink. (He later learned that the two men he saved had made it back to England, but that the one who was his friend was killed in Normandy in 1944.)

Curry spent five hours in the water after that. At one point, little fish began jumping around him. No, it was bullets hitting the surface. He swam to a landing craft that was idling in neutral and, grabbing onto ropes, hauled himself up the side, only to find it full of dead bodies.

The Germans opened up on him again, so he dived for safety. By then, he had stripped off his waterlogged clothes, was down to his underwear and ID tags. "I had my chocolate ration tucked in the band of my jockey shorts." Exhausted, he lay on a lifejacket and let the tide carry him. "I was in the water until five or six at night." He washed ashore under one of the towering cliffs that flank Dieppe. ("I saw a Spitfire and a German Messerschmitt slam into those cliffs. They were dogfighting and got too low.") It took him an hour to walk to a cleft in the rocks. The gully was packed with the bodies of dead Canadians, floating in the surf. Curry tried to see if his brother, Norman, was among them.

He figured he was lucky to be wearing nothing but underpants when a big German popped up and pointed a rifle at him.

"I'm sure if I'd been in uniform he would have shot me."

Marched into a factory where other prisoners were corralled, he found his brother, fast asleep. Norman began to cry when Ken woke him; he had been told Ken was dead. (In fact, their mother got a telegram to that effect, which put her in hospital for two weeks.) It was Norman who noticed the bullet crease down Ken's back. Ken didn't remember being wounded.

The prisoners spent three weeks in France before being loaded onto a train, eighty to a boxcar, and shipped to the Polish-German border and the notorious Stalag VIII-B. (Among the inmates was a single member of Britain's Home Guard, a man who had, after being sent for fish and chips by his wife in Brighton, been snatched off an English beach by a raiding party from a German U-boat.) Of Curry's two years and nine months as a POW, more than a year was spent in chains (though he learned to open his manacles with a sardine can key).

Once, a German officer with a glass eye jammed a Luger against Curry's head. Another of his jailers, a weasely little guy whom Curry could have snapped in two, laid a beating on him for singing "We're Going to Hang Out the Washing on the Siegfried Line." During a forced march at the end of the war, the prisoners, covered in fleas and lice, were reduced to living on boiled grain scavenged from barn floors.

Even the end of the fighting didn't really mean peace for some POWs. Many had health issues, both physical and psychological. "We all came out with one thing or another." Curry was among the better adjusted.

Still, it was hard not to be bitter.

"I lost three years of my life that I shouldn't have," Curry said. "We were sitting ducks."

That was three years without Norma, the girl from the northeast of England whom he had married just a week before the raid—not long enough to really get to know her, but long enough for her to become pregnant. It was an unconventional start to a marriage that lasted until her death in 2016.

It was the waste, the botched planning, that appalled him in 1942 and that still appalled him seventy-five years later. Never should have had a head-on attack in broad daylight, he said. Should have taken out the artillery beforehand. Should have taken out the machine guns in the hotels. Shouldn't have sent tanks onto a rocky beach where they would lose their treads.

Instead, after three years of training, the regiment was tossed into a buzz saw. "We were top soldiers, and in four hours there was nothing left. How the hell do you forget that?"

"I still remember everything very clearly about Dieppe and I probably will until the day I die," he said in 2017, preparing to head to Ontario to meet a friend for the seventy-fifth anniversary of the raid. Of the 582 soldiers of the Royal Hamilton Light Infantry who landed at Dieppe, they were the only two still alive. Almost two hundred had died on the beach. "I lost a lot of friends."

ALMOST ALL THE men mentioned here are gone now. Jim Vincent died in 2010, Earl Taylor in 2013. Doug Laurie also went in 2013, a year and a half after his hospital bed interview. Ken

Byron, as mentioned, died on his Salt Spring Island farm in 2014, but as of this writing, his kid brother, Terry, was hanging in on his own down-the-road farm at age ninety-six. I think sometimes of how Ken Byron was when I first met him—scarred by cancer, proud, independent—and contrast it with the youthful soldier in that fading army photo. As the years have passed, these old men's stories have faded, too, become black-and-white photos in a history text, not quite real to the rest of us.

Earl Clark died on Remembrance Day 2016, at age one hundred. When I spoke to his daughter Christine, she said she had grown up knowing about his physical scars—a German "potato masher" grenade blinded him for six weeks in 1945 and left him with shrapnel in one lung and behind one of his eyes for the rest of his life—but what she didn't know was how much he carried D-Day with him for all those years. Like so many of the veterans, he kept it to himself.

They were, as has often been said, Canada's Greatest Generation—raised in the Depression, robbed of their youth by war, then grateful for the chance to build a better life.

Meeting them, it was hard not to feel a little smaller, a little softer, a little less adequate in their presence.

TOP Terry and Ray Williams with their granddaughter Olivia (or K'wak'wat, meaning sea otter) at their home overlooking Yuquot, also known as Friendly Cove, on Nootka Island.
DEBRA BRASH/*TIMES COLONIST*

BOTTOM A fallen totem pole lies in the forest, just steps from the home of Terry and Ray Williams at Yuquot. DEBRA BRASH/
TIMES COLONIST

TOP Alban Michael beside a welcoming figure on the beach at Oclucje on northern Vancouver Island. DEBRA BRASH/*TIMES COLONIST*

BOTTOM Of the seven billion people on Earth, Alban Michael was the last to speak the Nuchatlaht language. DEBRA BRASH/*TIMES COLONIST*

TOP Richard Reiter in his Victoria home in 2005, with lithographs that were taken from Adolf Hitler's Berghof after it was bombed by Allied aircraft at the end of the Second World War. RAY SMITH/*TIMES COLONIST*

BOTTOM Kelly Carson at a rally protesting a deer cull in Oak Bay. Although she doesn't like using the bullhorn, Carson feels compelled to stand up for her beliefs. ADRIAN LAM/*TIMES COLONIST*

TOP, LEFT Victoria couple Julie and Colin Angus have carved a career out of seeking out adventure and documenting their feats of endurance in books and on film. RAY SMITH/*TIMES COLONIST*

TOP, RIGHT Tim Plakolli (left) and his cousins Artor and Visar Gashi (middle) pose with Hiep Nguyen (right) in front of the Gashis' barbershop and Nguyen's restaurant on Fort Street—two refugee-run small businesses in the heart of Victoria. Nguyen escaped from Vietnam in 1987, while the Gashi brothers were expelled from their native Kosovo in 1999. ADRIAN LAM/*TIMES COLONIST*

BOTTOM, LEFT Before he rose to prominence as a beloved philanthropist who has given millions of dollars to Victoria-area charities, Rudi Hoenson was a prisoner of war who survived the atomic bombing at Nagasaki. BRUCE STOTESBURY/*TIMES COLONIST*

BOTTOM, RIGHT "Every once in a while you wake up in the night and, boom, you're right there," says D-Day veteran Earl Clark. His retelling of that harrowing day on Juno Beach is devoid of any bravado or flag-waving. It is a stark picture of the terrors of war. BRUCE STOTESBURY/ *TIMES COLONIST*

LEFT Barry Campbell with beachcombing finds in Tofino, including some of his cherished Japanese glass fishing floats. DEBRA BRASH/ *TIMES COLONIST*

RIGHT "We wanted to be together all the time," says Larry Douglas, of his and his wife, Avril's, decision to spend their life in the remote lighthouse at Entrance Island. DEBRA BRASH/*TIMES COLONIST*

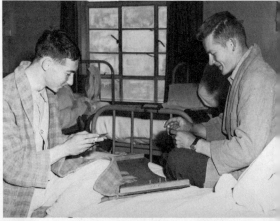

TOP, LEFT D-Day veteran Ken Byron in his home on Salt Spring Island. At age twenty-three, Byron had barely landed in France when he found himself in charge after his commanding officer was badly wounded. "I was platoon commander as soon as I hit the beach," Byron recalls. DEBRA BRASH/*TIMES COLONIST*

TOP, RIGHT Ken Byron (left) and Roger Schjelderup (right) play cards in a British hospital in 1944 after being wounded on D-Day. CANADIAN ARMY

BOTTOM, LEFT "The best way to break barriers is to establish yourself as competent at what you do," says Luc Cassivi. In the space of a generation, Cassivi's service as an openly gay base commander at CFB Esquimalt went from being grounds for expulsion from the Canadian Armed Forces to being a total non-issue. LYLE STAFFORD/*TIMES COLONIST*

BOTTOM, RIGHT When Constable Sarah Beckett was killed by a drunk driver in April 2016, the people of Greater Victoria responded with an outpouring of grief. At her funeral procession, shown here, a riderless horse led the hearse to the Q Centre, which was packed with 3,600 mourners. DARREN STONE/*TIMES COLONIST*

TOP, LEFT Mei Lee outside her sandwich shop, Orchard on View, which she opened in 2004 and has run singlehandedly ever since. ADRIAN LAM/*TIMES COLONIST*

TOP, RIGHT Andrea Sanborn, executive director of the U'mista Cultural Centre, was successful in repatriating a Kwakwaka'wakw transformation mask that was confiscated from an illegal potlatch and housed in the British Museum for decades. DEBRA BRASH/*TIMES COLONIST*

BOTTOM Bill Cranmer beside a decaying totem pole on Village Island, where, in 1921, his father hosted a potlatch that was raided by authorities. DEBRA BRASH/*TIMES COLONIST*

TOP Peter Knighton and his late wife, Monique, owners of Chez Monique. The world's least likely, most appreciated store and restaurant is located just south of Carmanah Point, halfway down the West Coast Trail and about three days from civilization. DEBRA BRASH/ *TIMES COLONIST*

BOTTOM, LEFT Being trapped atop the Johnson Street Bridge in 1953 has had a lasting effect on Peter Reitsma, shown here in his Saanich home, surrounded by his own artwork. "Still, today, I stay down close to earth," he says. ADRIAN LAM/*TIMES COLONIST*

BOTTOM, RIGHT As goodhearted as her name implies, Gladys Sweett turned 100 years old on September 6, 2017. Here, she takes a 100th-birthday carriage ride with her granddaughter Ashley and her dog, Maggie. DARREN STONE/*TIMES COLONIST*

no news is
good news

THE STORY WASN'T that Victoria's naval base, CFB Esquimalt, was waving goodbye to an openly gay base commander.

The story was that it isn't a story.

The story was that in the space of a generation, Commodore Luc Cassivi's homosexuality had gone from being grounds for expulsion from the Canadian Armed Forces to being totally irrelevant, grounds for nothing more than a shrug. That's a good thing.

I sat down with Cassivi one day in 2014 as he and partner Francisco Mejia De La Rosa were packing up, preparing to move to Ottawa, where Cassivi was about to become director general at National Defence Headquarters.

It was a far different navy from the one in which Cassivi enlisted in 1983, when gays and lesbians in the military were "very much deep in the closet," he said. Back then, a standing order stated that anyone suspected of homosexuality should be investigated and, if the allegation was proven, chucked out of the Forces.

"We had a special investigative unit, part of the military police, that was actively trying to find the folks who were so inclined and drive them out of the service," Cassivi said.

People like him stayed under the radar. "Those who were dedicated to the service, and who wanted to continue to serve, maintained two lives," he said. It meant putting up with a lot of crap that wouldn't be tolerated today. "There was a time that—call it bashing, call it bullying, call it a bad sense of humour—it was all there."

That wasn't just limited to the military, though. The same attitudes prevailed in the corporate world, even if the systemic discrimination wasn't codified. Whether it was in the wardroom or the boardroom, the derisive comments were the same. "It was like Newfie jokes. In those days, nobody had a second thought about saying those things."

The pendulum swung in 1992 when, following a court challenge by Michelle Douglas, who had been forced out of the air force in 1989, the Armed Forces cancelled the regulation banning gays and lesbians. While that makes it sound as though the bosses only moved because there was a judicial gun to their heads, there was in fact little resistance from those in power. The military might be rooted in tradition and conservative values, but by the early 1990s, the brass didn't need much persuading that change was needed.

"We had some great leaders who said, 'This is the Canadian thing to do, this is the right thing to do,'" Cassivi said.

It wasn't as though the entire culture of the Armed Forces changed with the stroke of a pen, though. Changes in institutional policy don't always occur in tandem with changes in people's beliefs. Sometimes the law has to play catch-up with a shift in public attitudes, and sometimes the attitudinal shift gets nudged along by the change in law. In the case of the military and homosexuality, the latter was the case. "The policy was ahead of culture in that era, but it was the right thing to do."

Despite the lifting of the ban, Cassivi wasn't sure the culture really would transform, or that he wanted to stay in the service if it didn't. Posted to the Royal Australian Navy for three years, he used the time away as a chance to see whether change would be accepted. Returning to Canada in 1997, he was pleased—though not really surprised—to see people had adapted. "Deep down, I had some faith, because I had seen the transformation when women joined the ranks."

He also knew that his colleagues weren't blind, that even before the ban was lifted, many of them knew who he was and supported him as a valued co-worker.

There's the key. "The best way to break barriers is to establish yourself as competent at what you do," he says. Either you can do the job or not. Either your co-workers can count on you or not. After that, the other facets of who you are—race, gender, sexual preference—become secondary. Cassivi has been in charge of three submarines, a frigate, and a naval base; what else do you need to know?

If this seems blindingly obvious today, years after an openly gay Anglican priest became head chaplain of the Canadian Armed Forces and years after same-sex marriage became a non-issue in Canada, well, that wasn't always the case. It was only in 2005 that Canada became just the fourth country in the world to make same-sex marriage legal nationwide.

In 2000, when I was the *Times Colonist*'s opinion pages editor, I went to our then publisher, Peter Baillie, and told him I wanted to write an editorial in which the newspaper would endorse same-sex marriage. No big deal today, but back then it was like asking him to walk off a cliff. Peter, who would bear the consequences of any fallout, looked as though he had been punched. Then he took a deep breath and said, "It's going to cost us readers and it's going to cost us advertisers, but it's the right thing to do. Do it."

I always admired him for that, because back then it took courage. Note that when *Times Colonist* reporter Cindy Harnett wrote a positive account of the unlicensed marriage of a Victoria lesbian couple that summer, an editor pushed her story inside the paper, declaring, "Our readers don't want to see that sort of thing on the front page on a Sunday morning." He was right: many didn't. Some still don't; beliefs can't be turned on and off with a switch.

The thing is, Harnett's piece wouldn't even get written today, because it's no longer news.

Sometimes a non-story is the best story of all.

bondo

═══

THEY SAY BONDO has a photographic memory. He claims it's fading now, but thirteen years after turning in his badge, he spits out names, dates, and addresses with the rat-a-tat chatter of an old-fashioned tickertape.

Still, the legendary Doug Bond, the Bobby Orr of street cops, can't be expected to remember all seventy thousand of the calls he handled over three decades, a Code 3 career that finally lights-and-sirened to a screeching halt in 2005.

Flipping through the Bond file is like reading a movie script, or maybe a Joseph Wambaugh novel. Here he is racing into a burning rooming house to drag a man out of his apartment. Here he is giving mouth-to-mouth to a fifteen-year-old girl about to die of a heroin overdose. Here he is plucking children from a flame-engulfed boat, or rescuing drowning kids from Beaver Lake, or resuscitating a man who's had a heart attack behind the wheel.

His size 14s have booted more doors than a rodeo bull. He has investigated hundreds of sexual assaults, child-abuse cases, murders. He has broken his hand, busted his nose, suffered four concussions, been knocked unconscious when struck by a vehicle, and once had his motorcycle run over by a driver who dragged him for three lanes under her car. Other cops called him the best they had ever known.

What's really strange is that in a profession famous for chewing up, burning out, and embittering those who stay too long, Sergeant Doug Bond remained upbeat, garrulous, and gregarious, right to the end. He's still that way.

"I've never seen his expression change," said dispatcher Isabelle McHardy as Bond prepared to pull the plug. "He's always so damn cheerful. He tells you stories and he talks so fast you can't tell what he's saying."

Doug Bond was born in Vancouver but moved at age five to Victoria, where his dad was in the car business and his mother had a gift shop. He attended Catholic schools—Sacred Heart, St. Louis College—before going to Saanich's Reynolds Secondary and Camosun College. Drove tow truck for Tolmie Towing for three years, mostly clearing car crashes, which is where he started getting friendly with cops.

One day, while enjoying a few cocktails—okay, maybe more than a few—at the Red Lion Inn, Bond was persuaded by accident investigator Pete Talavs to join the boys in blue. On February 1, 1975, he signed on with the Victoria Police. It wouldn't happen today: "They don't hire nineteen-year-olds anymore."

His first call was to a boat in distress off Clover Point. His second was to an overdose. The overdose victim lived—Bond found himself dealing with the same guy at a fight just before he retired, more than thirty years later.

He worked traffic, was in an organized-crime unit, sleuthed as a detective, and did five years on the major crimes squad, but his first love was patrol, being a street cop. "It's all the action calls," he said, slipping behind the wheel of a Chevy Tahoe for his last night shift before retirement. Sometimes it's boom-boom-boom all shift, flitting from domestic dispute to car crash to burglary to mental-health call to wrestling-on-the-sidewalk pandemonium. You need versatility for this job. Or maybe attention deficit disorder.

On his last night, Bond had a little more time for reflection, though it was still busy enough, as a record of the evening shows:

▶ **7:20 PM**—Bond spots two girls duking it out at Douglas and Yates. The kids hightail it as he hits the brakes, but Bond manages to halt one of the girls. A couple of shaken Californian tourists say she was getting the hell kicked out of her by the other girl and a guy who had pulled a honking big knife. Within moments the intersection is bathed in blue and red lights as more units respond, but the other combatants are nowhere to be found. The teenager Bond collared isn't badly hurt and won't co-operate with police. "It'll be a drug deal or sex-trade workers fighting over turf," says Bond.

▶ **7:30 PM**—An obnoxious drunk at the legislature—or, to be precise, an unelected obnoxious drunk at the legislature—is making threats, so gets hauled away to sleep it off. No point in charging him. He won't remember the threats in the morning.

▶ **8:30 PM**—A man complains of being bitten by a pit bull. The owner blames the dog's unhappy childhood. Animal Control is called, though you get the impression Bond feels worse about jailing dogs than people. At home, the Bonds have four dogs—two Newfoundlanders, two golden retrievers—whom he calls "my kids."

▶ **8:49 PM**—Lights and sirens to Store Street, where a man is convulsing on the sidewalk. The fellow who saw him fall says the guy reeks of booze. Other emergency vehicles arrive, and the man is whisked away by ambulance. A firefighter extends his hand to Bond. "Your last night? It's been a pleasure working with you." Paramedics echo the sentiment. Bond is famous for getting emergency agencies to work together. He likes them and they like him.

▶ **9:17 PM**—More lights and sirens down Yates Street, faster than you've ever dreamed of driving downtown, where a drunken shoplifter has gotten into it with staff at the Market on Yates. Bond briskly cuffs the guy and marches him out. Shoplifters are usually catch-and-release, but this one was making threats and has a record that includes assault, robbery, grievous bodily harm—so the police will hold him for court.

Drug users, particularly those in the grips of crystal meth and cocaine psychosis, have made the streets meaner than they used to be. Even shoplifters carry knives. Mental-health calls became common after the province shut down the institutions and turned the afflicted onto the street. On Bond's last night shift, his watch picks up fifteen people under the Mental Health Act. "We're a fast-response social agency, 24/7."

▶ **FAST-FORWARD TO 1 AM**—More social service work: while looking for a man who assaulted a clerk at the Mega-Mart on Gorge Road, Bond spots an old man working on a bottle of Listerine. Bond knows the guy, who lives under a bridge by the Galloping Goose trail. "Do you want to go to the station or go there?" Bond asks after pouring out the Listerine. The guy, who is blotto, opts for a ride to a friend's place. "Nice car," he observes, climbing in the back.

▶ **2:15 AM**—On Humboldt Street, a whacked-out young man appears to have done a header off a bicycle. He seems unaware that his money and hash pipe are on the sidewalk. A package of cocaine emerges from his pocket. He is one of the Victoria Police Department's frequent flyers—the department has dealt with him an impressive 162 times in his young life. Bond calls the man by his first name. Watching the two of them is like watching the Bugs Bunny cartoon where the wolf and sheepdog punch the clock together.

There was no more clock-punching once Bond called it a day—and, thankfully, no more dealing with death, the constant companion of patrol sergeants, who are required to show up any time someone expires outside a hospital. Bond can only guess at the number—from heart attacks, car crashes, murders, whatever—he attended. The oldest was ninety-eight, the youngest fourteen days old. Bond performed CPR on the latter for seven minutes but it didn't work.

He dealt with maybe two hundred suicides, including those of two colleagues. The suicides he found sadder than the murders, the deceased's state of mind coming into play. He genuinely cared about these people, even called the newspaper once to express his disgust with a mob that had gathered by the Johnson Street Bridge, where a mentally ill man was threatening to leap. "Jump!" they called. "Jump, you chickenshit!" And the man almost did. "You could see he was getting psyched up to go over the edge," Bond said. When one of the rubberneckers got too close, loud, and insistent, the police chased him down and led him away in handcuffs. The distraught man was talked off the bridge, but Bond was still upset the next day.

Sometimes things turn out great. The would-be jumper is talked out of it. The fifteen-year-old responds to CPR. "When you save people, it's a pretty nice feeling."

Still, negativity is at the heart of police work. "Nobody ever calls you because they're happy."

Bond should be cynical and twisted, but he isn't. "I've always had a pretty good outlook," he says. Being a strong Catholic, going to church every week, helped. So did sitting on the deck with his dogs, working his way through a few beer, back in the old days. Sometimes, when things got too much, he would go to Vancouver and get a hotel room where he could just zone out on the balcony, watching planes take off and land at the airport, one after another.

And Cory, with whom he is clearly smitten, is a strength. She joined the Victoria Police in 1985. She was Inspector Cory Bond, the highest-ranking woman in the department, when she joined Doug in retirement in 2010. Doug's brother John was also on the Victoria force. Cory's sister was with the Central Saanich department.

Cory says Doug has time for everyone, treats everyone fairly, no matter who they are. In 1987, he sparked an international incident by going after an American sailor whom he wanted to charge with assaulting a sex-trade worker. Bond went nose-to-nose with the sailor's captain, who blocked the cop from the ship, but Bond kept pressing until the story made the national news in Canada and the US. The sailor was eventually tried and acquitted, but the prostitute didn't forget Bond's efforts. She later became instrumental in solving a murder.

All these years later, Bond's stories remain funny (though they're funnier when delivered in his machine-gun staccato).

He once told the suspect in a credit union robbery that the man matched the description given by the tellers. "That's bullshit," the man replied. "I had my face covered."

He has another tale about a hard-luck burglar who crashed through the ceiling of the old police club on Pembroke Street, spilling the drinks of the officers below. He remembers a bunch of drunks stealing another drunk's artificial leg, and still another who made off with the light bar from a police car. One thief cleaned out an ambulance—stretcher, oxygen, defibrillator, the works—only to return it after Bond tracked him down and said, "You might hate cops, but these paramedics bust their butts for people like you." No charges were laid.

Then there was the dry cleaner who would occasionally "lose" officers' garments. By the time he was caught, the dry cleaner had assembled an entire uniform, piece by piece. "I was jealous," Bond says. "He looked better in uniform than I did."

He was driving by the Johnson Street Bridge one night when he saw a pedestrian staring up into the ironwork. "Uh-oh," he thought, "there's a jumper." Actually, it was a humper—two of them, in fact, copulating way up where they thought no one would see them. Bond called up, "Haven't you ever heard of safe sex? Get down here." They did.

The stories about Bondo are as colourful as the ones he tells. Cory recalls dropping him off at church one day, figuring it was the one place he couldn't find trouble. Wrong. When she returned to St. Andrew's Cathedral, the blue-and-reds were flashing outside, the congregation milling about on the sidewalk. Somebody had rushed the altar to attack the priest, but Bondo had shot out of his pew and clotheslined the guy as he bolted up the aisle. The two men ended up rolling out the door and down the steps, the dispute ending with the cop on top. Even the chief cracked up when he heard about that one.

Some of Bondo's stories still ricochet around the department today. One has to do with a wild house party that the police broke up by grabbing the partiers and firing them out the door. One young man pointed a warning finger at Bond: "My uncle is a lawyer."

"That right?" replied the policeman. "My uncle has a border collie."

"What's that got to do with anything?" the man asked.

"Exactly," replied Bond, seizing the man and throwing him into the night.

Can't do that sort of thing anymore. It's a different world today. Bond figures he got out at the right time. Policing is much more process-driven now, with less discretion to employ street smarts or common sense when dealing with people.

When Bond started his career, his uniform belt held a five-shot .38 calibre pistol and a set of handcuffs. By the time he packed it in, the list had expanded to include a 9-millimetre Glock, extra ammo, cuffs, a radio, telescoping baton, pepper spray, Taser, Maglite, pouch with latex gloves, and on and on. Bond, like one of those old-time hockey players who couldn't get used to a helmet, shunned the protective vests that all cops now wear.

In 1975, his cruiser carried a small first aid kit and fire extinguisher. Thirty years later his supervisor's vehicle came with a computer at his right elbow and carried an assault rifle, beanbag-firing shotgun, door-spreaders, heavy body armour, crime-scene kits, rappelling harnesses for retrieving bridge-jumpers, face masks for entering clandestine drug labs, duffel bag stuffed with medical gear, jumbo-sized container of pepper spray—"manners in a can"—and a whole range of fire extinguishers.

Today he shudders at the other burdens of modern policing. Technology and disclosure requirements make documenting even the simplest of investigations a never-ending exercise, turning street cops into desk jockeys. In public, there's always someone with a phone camera in your face.

Not that Bond ever shied from scrutiny. Far from it. The news media loved him because he believed in being open, figuring the more access reporters had, the greater their understanding would be. Ask him a question, he answered, probably after beckoning the cameras through the door he had just booted. That attitude wouldn't fly in today's culture of carefully controlled message management.

So, yes, plenty of journalists showed up at his retirement bash, along with several hundred cops, paramedics, prosecutors, defence lawyers, firefighters, judges, politicians, and the servers from the Paul's Motor Inn restaurant, site of innumerable middle-of-the-night coffee breaks. "Personally," said his old friend McHardy, "I don't think anyone will ever fill his shoes." She was right.

Today, Bond sounds the same. He's still nocturnal, a news junkie, devours newspapers, staying up late flipping news channels.

He looks different, though. He has lost fifty pounds and fifty years since leaving the force. His lifestyle is healthier. He eats fish, but no other meat, changing his diet following a cross-country drive in which he watched truck after truck hauling livestock to slaughter. Cory is the same.

In fact, animal welfare is their passion. The Bonds are big defenders of dogs—the older, uglier, and more gimped-up, the better. They adopt the broken and abused animals that no one else wants, smother them in affection in their final days, see them slip off to Puppy Heaven, then do it again.

They take in the likes of Elmer, a big, black, aging fellow who was found eating out of garbage cans in Oakland, California. With a club foot and some badly healed injuries that left him lurching like a peg-legged pirate, Elmer was considered unadoptable, and was an hour from being put down when rescued; the Bonds took him home after travelling to California for another dog, a blind one. Among their other adoptees was a border collie that had been left tied to a railing in Hinton, Alberta, and another that had suffered caustic burns after being stranded in a manure pit. Others had cancer, hearing loss, or damaged joints.

The Bonds once took in a springer spaniel whose name Doug changed to Jerry. "He's eleven," Cory said. "You can't change his name." "Cory, he's deaf," Doug replied.

At least Jerry moved better than Chevy, who needed to be carried down the stairs to Doug's Tavern, the man cave in the basement of their home. They used to have some great Super Bowl parties down there. Used to. After the league welcomed back Michael Vick, the quarterback convicted of running a dog-fighting ring, NFL football was banned from the house. The Bonds finally relented and watched the 2018 championship game after reading stories of NFL players taking in rescue dogs.

Taking in dogs comes at a high cost, financially and emotionally. The Bonds—who also spend a lot on children in poorer countries through a church program—have spent $300,000 caring for their animals. They also have urns holding the ashes of twenty-seven dogs, each of whom lives on in a photographic memory.

sarah beckett

TEN, TWENTY, THIRTY years from now, this is what Sarah Beckett's boys can take away from her funeral: their mother mattered.

That's good, because strip away all of the pageantry—the ranks of red serge, the bagpipes, the flag-draped coffin—and what was left was a picture of a thirty-two-year-old who loved her family intensely. Beckett died April 5, 2016, in Langford when her marked RCMP car was broadsided by a pickup truck at 3:30 AM.

People in Greater Victoria greeted her death with an outpouring of genuine grief, one that culminated a week later when thousands lined the Old Island Highway to watch her fellow police officers march to her memorial service in Colwood. Others watched or listened live on television, radio, and online.

The Q Centre was packed with 3,600 mourners, most of them in uniform. Just up the hill at the Juan de Fuca Recreation Centre, another 200 watched a live feed on a big screen, while a similar number did the same a few kilometres away at Westhills Stadium.

Had it been a civilian whose car was broadsided, would there have been such a reaction? No, there wouldn't, but civilians don't spend eleven years keeping the rest of us safe in our beds, as Beckett did as a member of the RCMP. And yes, it was heartbreaking that she should be snatched from her husband and their five- and two-year-old sons.

The circumstances of her death finally came out in 2017: a drunk driver, his blood-alcohol three times the legal limit, was doing between seventy-six and ninety kilometres an hour when he ran a red light and struck the police car broadside in the intersection. Beckett was simply in the wrong place at the wrong time. The driver was sentenced to four years in prison.

Everyone—not just the tightly knit policing family—seemed to want to play a part in remembering Beckett. By the day of the service, hundreds of bouquets of flowers, bordered by candles burning in the rain, had been left outside Beckett's West Shore detachment. A GoFundMe campaign for the family had topped eighty thousand dollars. Rec centre staff had trimmed the foliage around the Q Centre, wanting the scene of the funeral to look good.

The funeral procession shut down the Juan de Fuca centre—the pool, library, and gym—and cut access to nearby businesses, but no one seemed to mind. Across the road, Saunders Subaru cleared all the cars off its front lot to make room for mourners' vehicles and placed Beckett's regimental number—51939—on its marquee. Nearby, the Galaxy Motors sign read RIP CONST. BECKETT.

"Showing up here as a community is important," said Esquimalt's Marilyn Day. Clad in red, she didn't know Beckett but was first in line outside the Q Centre at 8:30 AM, five and a half hours before the funeral. "I wanted to say thanks for keeping us safe. We should do that more often."

The procession up the Old Island Highway was a spectacle.

Onlookers applauded the lead RCMP motorcycle riders as they turned into the Juan de Fuca grounds, and they clapped when pipers wheeled past playing "Green Hills/Battle's O'er."

But when the hearse appeared, preceded by a riderless horse with Beckett's boots backward in the stirrups, they fell silent. When the Mounties who knew Beckett best—her troopmates from Regina, and those who had worked with her at West Shore and the Vancouver Island Integrated Major Crime Unit—marched past, some in tears, all in red serge, the only sound was that of the hard soles of high brown boots hitting the pavement in unison.

That sound changed to a muffled thud when Greater Victoria's municipal police came past in their softer-bottomed boots. Then came more red serge and more municipal dark blue, punctuated by unfamiliar uniforms from far-off places— the green of the US Border Patrol, the bright blue of the Winnipeg Police. Firefighters and paramedics also made a strong showing.

This family is tight. "It's very important to us to be here," said Patrolman Josh Wilson of the Bellingham Police. BC Ferries said four hundred first responders sailed to Vancouver Island on the morning of the funeral.

(Also note that Saanich police officers covered for the West Shore RCMP day shift so that the latter could attend the funeral. Duncan/North Cowichan Mounties took the night watch. Central Saanich police covered for Sidney/ North Saanich RCMP and VicPD officers took shifts in Sooke. Officers working overtime donated their pay to Beckett's family.)

For others, the motivation was purely personal. Mitch Conner, twenty-three, came down from Nanaimo. His mother and Sarah's mother are friends, so he saw Sarah often while growing up. As a preteen, he looked forward to trips to their house. "Sarah always had something fun planned. She would set up these epic games of hide and seek." Or maybe they would play *Donkey Kong Country* on a Super Nintendo. "She was wickedly funny."

That was a common description. People kept talking about how funny she was, how well liked she was. Apparently, she could do a seagull imitation that could even confuse a seagull. There was a story about how she got tagged with the nickname Back-up Beckett after reversing a cruiser into a fire truck in Port McNeill, her first posting after becoming a Mountie in 2005.

Beckett's godfather, Jack Hayden, told the assemblage about a girl who moved to Victoria from Alberta during elementary school, progressing from Hampton Elementary to Colquitz Junior and Belmont Secondary before graduating from Spectrum. She dreamed of becoming a paleontologist (she saw *Jurassic Park* fourteen times) before shifting her focus to the RCMP.

As a mother, and as a daughter of an Indo-Canadian mother, Beckett knew she represented the new face of the force and was serious about being a good officer, Hayden said.

And, indeed, she was a terrific police officer, Staff Sergeant Phil Lue—her boss in Port McNeill—told the funeral. It was no surprise when she made the major crime unit in 2009, getting transferred home to Victoria. But more than being good at her job, she was a good person. "She was kind, generous, sweet, loyal, and loving," said Lue.

Her boys—born in 2011 and 2014—and husband, Brad Aschenbrenner, benefited from that. "Sarah loved her family, thrived on being a wife and mother," Lue said.

That message was repeated again and again. Hayden said it, too.

He also read out a message to Sarah from her husband, Brad: "You warned me this day may come when we first met each other, but I was not prepared for it. I want you to know that even if I would have known this would happen when we first met, I would still have taken this journey a thousand times over with you."

mei lee

A BUSINESS TURNING fourteen years old wouldn't normally be that remarkable, particularly when it's a tiny little shop run by a tiny little woman eking out a living one sandwich at a time.

But when the woman is a sweet-natured immigrant like Mei Lee, navigating life without a map, all alone in the world save for the son she raised on her own, the milestone is worth a mention.

That map analogy is Lee's own. She really has had to be her own guide, working, working, working to scratch out a life in the Orchard on View, the closet of a place that she runs all by herself on the View Street side of Victoria's Bay Centre. It's where we met her in 2009 when just-getting-by downtown businesses were jeopardized by a spate of late-night drunken window-smashing. A five-hundred-dollar insurance deductible is a fortune when you're only making thirty cents, fifty cents, on a sale.

Yet there she was in March 2018, still hanging in, giving out slices of cake to customers to celebrate another year in business.

Not that it's easy to last in a town with a soup-and-sandwich spot on every corner. Nothing has come easily to Mei Lee.

Lee didn't finish elementary school in Singapore, couldn't read or write Mandarin, let alone English, when she landed in Calgary, where an uncle lived, in 1977. She was twenty-one.

"At that time, I don't know English at all," she says.

She washed dishes in a Calgary hotel, married a man from Hong Kong, gave birth to a boy, Ray, in 1981.

"The marriage don't work out, so I've been on my own since my son is a year and a half."

She met a Newfoundlander who told her St. John's would be a good place to raise Ray, so moved there for six years, making pizzas for a living. When it became obvious that Newfoundlanders were looking west for their future, she decided that would be the best thing for Ray, too, and headed to Victoria in 1991.

Alerted by a friend in Newfoundland, a nun from the Sisters of St. Ann met Lee at the Victoria bus depot and took her to the Douglas Hotel, where mother and son lived for three weeks until low-cost housing opened up. Lee washed dishes at the naval dockyard for six months, then got work picking strawberries at Oldfield Orchard on the Saanich Peninsula. She toiled there for twelve years, picking berries and apples in the fields, moving to the farm's roadside market as her English improved.

She opened Orchard on View in 2004. "It take me a long time to save a little bit of money to open this store." The occasion was reported in a *Times Colonist* newspaper column, a framed copy of which hangs in her window today.

Lee wanted to be a fruit vendor, but her landlady said she would need the lunch trade to survive. "It was very scary," she says. "At the beginning, I don't know how to make a fancy sandwich, but the people still come."

She rises at 5 AM, heads to the bakery, then arrives at the shop by 7 or so, six days a week. She closes up at 6 PM, then goes grocery shopping. On Sundays she sleeps in a bit, but still gets up in time to go to church, then Costco, then to Orchard on View to get ready for the week. She's a bit wistful about having had to pass up chances to go to school, but there was no time. Now in her sixties, her feet let her know that she spends all day, every day, standing behind her display case. Her bones let her know about all those hours bent over the counter, making sandwiches.

Here's what makes it a story: after all this, she is profoundly grateful.

"I want to say a big thank you to Canada that I have this opportunity."

She is thankful to the Newfoundland neighbours who shovelled her walk when it snowed. She is thankful to Oldfield Orchard for hiring her. She is thankful that Ray worked hard in school, earned a business degree, gave back as president of the Burnside Gorge Community Association. "As a parent, all I want is him to be a good Canadian citizen." He's working in Manhattan now, but she thinks he'll come home eventually.

She is thankful for the downtown retailers, lawyers, and civil servants who are her regulars. Hers isn't the only sandwich shop downtown and she's not the only hard-working immigrant, but after spending all those years watching Lee sweat for every inch of this tiny shop, they are grateful for her, too.

inseparable

$$\overline{\overline{}}$$

AFTER SIXTY-THREE YEARS of marriage, Helen and Bill Wilson died within a day of each other, just before Christmas in 2003.

It was sad in the way that any death is sad, particularly at that time of year, but also, said their son Jack, the end of a true love story.

Helen Maguire and Bill Wilson both grew up in Vancouver, but it was in Qualicum, where their families kept summer cabins, that they met as teenagers in the 1920s. "They used to play baseball in the sand," said Jack.

Helen was beautiful, athletic, and smart—she enrolled at the University of British Columbia at age sixteen and graduated at nineteen. "It was at a time when not a lot of women went to UBC," Jack said.

She was a good basketball player, an alternate for Canada's Olympic team in the 1930s. Jack didn't discover this until he himself was a teenaged player, practising outside the family home.

His mother came outside, took the ball, and began lobbing shots at the basket. "Swish, swish, five in a row," Jack recalled. "She said, 'It's easy when you know what you're doing,' and then she walked back into the kitchen."

Bill and Helen married in 1940, a few years after he got his medical degree, and just before he shipped out overseas with the army's 13 Field Ambulance. He served in Sicily, Italy, and Holland, coming back to Canada with the rank of major and an appointment to the Order of the British Empire. A distinguished career as a Vancouver eye surgeon and ophthalmologist followed, including a term as president of the Canadian Ophthalmological Society. "He was a Victorian gentleman. Nobody ever said a bad word about him," said Jack.

Helen was mother not only to sons Jack and David, but to the whole neighbourhood. Their home was a "clubhouse," a refuge for all. "She was just a very welcoming person."

In 1979, the Wilsons semi-retired to Qualicum Beach, where their romance had begun, and where it continued unabated. "They didn't hold hands a lot, but they respected each other."

They lived in the community for almost a quarter century. Bill was ninety-four when he died, Helen ninety-two. Both were mentally alert to the end. Even after Helen barely survived an aneurysm—and the amputation of her lower leg— eleven years earlier, the Wilsons remained in their own house.

It wasn't until the April of their last spring that they moved into a care home. Bill was healthy enough to stay behind at their house but didn't want to leave Helen's side. "He went purely out of devotion to her," said Jack.

Bill was the most robust person there, even if he could no longer indulge his twin passions of golf and gardening.

Two Sundays before Christmas, the Wilsons were their usual selves. Bill even gave Jack gardening tips before dinner. "He showed me how to trim the roses."

But within a couple of days, Bill fell ill with the flu. On Friday, he was taken to hospital in Nanaimo. That night, as Helen spoke to Jack, she began referring to her husband in the past tense and talked about how much she would miss Bill. Somehow she realized it was the end.

Six hours later, Helen Wilson died in her sleep.

"I truly believe that she knew that she couldn't live without him," said Jack. Helen needed Bill physically—to care for her, to brush her hair—and emotionally. "She knew that she didn't want to live without him."

In the morning, Jack went to the hospital to give his dad the news. But Bill was a bit delirious, so his son held back, speaking to his father of other things instead.

"At one point he said to me, 'Jack, get a chair for your mother.'

"I said, 'Why?'

"He said, 'She's standing in the doorway.'" Bill could see her clearly.

Jack never did tell his father that Helen had died the night before. The next day, Bill Wilson was gone, too.

reclaiming the past

BILL CRANMER PICKS his way along the path through the blackberry bushes, stepping over the piles of fresh bear scat, skirting the empty, falling-down houses of Village Island, finally arriving at a totem pole decaying at the water's edge. This is the scene of the crime.

Cranmer is chief of the 'Namgis First Nation, one of the Kwakwaka'wakw—or Kwak'wala-speaking—peoples whose traditional territory stretches from Comox in the south to the northern tip of Vancouver Island and the isolated islands and mainland inlets across the strait.

The 'Namgis are found at Alert Bay on Cormorant Island, a forty-five-minute ferry ride from Port McNeill, but on this day Cranmer has travelled across to the Broughton Archipelago and the isolated, long-uninhabited Indigenous community of 'Mimkwamlis—Village Island—where, in December 1921, his father threw a potlatch, setting in motion a cultural struggle that continues today.

It's a story that goes back to 1884, when the Canadian government banned the potlatch. Potlatches—long, elaborate ceremonies with feasts, speeches, ritual songs, and dances—marked marriages, births, deaths, pole-raisings, the bestowing of names, the passing of a chief's privileges, and more. History was passed down, social status validated, relations between tribes sorted out. Potlatches were an essential part of Indigenous life.

That's why Ottawa made them illegal: it believed banning the ceremony would speed Indigenous assimilation into white society. It was the same reasoning the residential schools used when punishing students caught speaking Indigenous languages.

But the potlatch did not die. Like the early Christian church, it just went underground, the singing and dancing going on in places where the authorities were unlikely to watch.

So Chief Dan Cranmer—Bill's dad—thought it was safe when he held a potlatch on isolated Village Island that December. "The potlatch went on for five or six days," says Bill Cranmer. The gifts included gas-powered boats, pool tables, cash, blankets, flour. "It was apparently one of the biggest potlatches ever held in our area."

Alas, word got out, the potlatch got busted, and forty-five people were arrested. Half of them, convicted of such crimes as dancing, making speeches, and accepting gifts, served two to three months at Burnaby's Oakalla Prison. The other twenty-two were freed on the condition that their people surrender all their potlatch paraphernalia—masks, whistles, rattles, headdresses, the works. In all, more than three hundred pieces were seized.

That's when the real crime happened, the 'Namgis say. Instead of being held in trust as promised, their artifacts were scattered among museums and private collections around the world. Most were shipped east, ending up in Toronto's Royal Ontario Museum and what is now the Canadian Museum of History in Ottawa. Other pieces ended up in private collections—thirty-three bought by New York collector George Heye went to the National Museum of the American Indian, now part of the Smithsonian.

By the time the potlatch ban faded away in 1951, the masks and rattles were scattered all over. The effect, says Bill Cranmer, was devastating, beyond what non-Indigenous people might expect. The damage was even worse than that wrought by the residential school system. "What they did was stop our ability to pass on our history." This was big-time stuff in a culture that puts such emphasis on handing down family possessions—masks, dances, songs, names, blanket designs— from generation to generation.

The Kwakwaka'wakw never stopped trying to reclaim the pieces they had given up under duress, arguing the items never should have been seized, let alone scattered to the wind. Retrieval of the lost treasures was seen as a way to honour those who had kept the culture alive, holding potlatches even when it might mean going to jail.

Some of the museums that held the artifacts were sympathetic, others not. For three decades beginning in the 1970s, the paraphernalia came trickling back. The National Museum of Man—now the Canadian Museum of History—was the first to return its items. The Royal Ontario Museum followed suit in 1988 and the National Museum of the American Indian beginning in 1994. The Potlatch Collection, as it is known, is shared and displayed by the U'mista Cultural Centre in Alert Bay and the Nuyumbalees Cultural Centre on Quadra Island.

It is believed that almost all the artifacts have been found and returned, though the absence of definitive records makes it hard to be certain. One story gives hope that even more will be recovered, though: in 2003, a *yaxwiwe'*, or headdress, came all the way from Paris, having been discovered in the apartment of the late French surrealist writer and visual artist André Breton.

Breton, as leader of the Surrealist movement (it emphasizes the irrational and the automatic over logic and reason), was a cultural icon in France. Many there viewed his apartment and its massive collection—several thousand pieces, including paintings by Salvador Dali, Joan Miró, and René Magritte—as something of a national shrine, and were upset when the government declined to preserve it.

Unpopular as that decision might have been (when the collection was broken up and sold, fetching $70 million, protesters threw stink bombs outside the Paris hotel where the auction was held), it also led to the return of the *yaxwiwe'*. The headdress features what is likely a raven carved out of wood, sitting above a hawk-like figure. The carving sits over the forehead and is held in place by an ermine band topped with sea lion whiskers. An ermine cape once flowed down the back, but not much remained of that. The dancer wearing the *yaxwiwe'* would place the down of an eagle inside the crown. When the dancer shook his head, the down would float away, symbolizing peace.

Breton may or may not have known all that, but French anthropologist Marie Mauzé certainly did. In 2003, having been asked to examine the headdress for possible purchase by the Louvre, she immediately recognized it as Kwakwaka'wakw, then discovered it was one of the missing potlatch pieces. Breton, Mauzé discovered, was just the last in a series of people who had bought the piece after it was "deaccessioned" by the National Museum of the American Indian. She told Breton's daughter, Aube Breton-Elléouët, who decided it should not be sold with the rest of the art.

Instead, the chic Parisienne returned it to Alert Bay, where she appeared both thrilled and bewildered when asked to join in a dance in the Big House, cedar smoke swirling around her.

"It was very important to my father," she said that day. "It was always on his desk, facing his chair. He had great admiration for American and Canadian Indians, the Indians of la Colombie-Britannique." She said she was happy to return it. When she did so, Bill Cranmer presided at the ceremony.

The return of the _yaxwiwe'_ was easier than the recovery of one other item, a transformation mask that the British Museum resolutely refused to let go.

Arguably the best-known museum on the planet, the London institution owns several thousand items related to Canadian Indigenous heritage, including woven cedar hats and a mask brought back by Captain James Cook, plus weapons and jewellery picked up by Captain George Vancouver. That left many wondering why it would care about a single mask, one that was packed away in storage at that.

The museum's reply was that its governing legislation, an act of the British parliament, specifically prohibited it from giving up artifacts. Others noted there was a significant queue of claimants wanting the return of items in the museum's possession, notably Greece's Elgin Marbles, taken from the Parthenon in the early 1800s, and eleven wooden tablets representing the original Ark of the Covenant, sacred to Ethiopia's 36 million Orthodox Christians, picked up by British soldiers later in the nineteenth century.

"My job is to preserve the collection we have, not to remove objects," the museum's then director, Robert Anderson, said in 2002. "My job is also to arrange for the presentation of world cultures to the 5 million people a year who come here."

Anderson maintained that the mask, bought from an American museum decades ago, had been obtained legally. Still, the British Museum found itself in an uncomfortable position. The David-versus-Goliath struggle was even detailed in *The New York Times*.

The David was personified by Andrea Sanborn, executive director of the U'mista Cultural Centre. A five-foot-nothing middle-aged woman from a tiny island town, hers might not have been the most intimidating presence when she travelled to London to insist on the repatriation of the artifact—but looks can be deceiving. Sanborn, her mother from the Ma'amtagila band of the Kwakwaka'wakw, her commercial fisherman father a first-generation Canadian of Ukrainian descent, was absolutely unrelenting in her quest for the mask.

She displayed the same backbone she had shown as a pioneer of Indigenous tourism in BC, which she believed in but—and this is important—only when it was done right. She was both a cheerleader for and guardian of her Kwakwaka'wakw culture, eager to display it to the world, but only in an uncorrupted form. "She was adamant about that," said her sister, Lillian Hunt. No way would Sanborn tolerate the Disneyfied ethno-schlock that gets sold as authentic native fare to daiquiri-sucking tourists elsewhere around the globe. Sanborn was a stickler for accuracy.

She could be stubborn as a bad cold when it came to protecting Indigenous culture—so it's a good thing that she had a sly sense of humour, too. It took the edge off confrontations, of which she had more than a few.

Once, she showed up at the British Museum with an empty Adidas bag.

"What's that for?" the perplexed museum boffins asked.

"I've come for the mask," she deadpanned.

The Brits weren't sure how to take that. It must have been hard for her to keep a straight face.

Sanborn wouldn't give up, kept plodding away with an approach both stubborn and disarming. (Note that Kwakwaka'wakw culture includes a "laugher dance," says Hunt. "We use our humour to take the sting out of getting what we want.")

She finally turned the tide by telling the British Museum brass that they shouldn't equate returning the mask with feeling guilty or admitting it was illegally in their possession. That worked. Sanborn won them over, even formed some lasting friendships with some of the British Museum representatives.

In 2005, the museum returned the transformation mask—one that opens up to change from one figure into another—on long-term loan.

All of which leads to the obvious question: Why bother? Why are so many Indigenous people focused on questions of culture and identity? The answer may lie in the fact that the culture was systematically repressed for so long—and the fact that it takes such a relentless effort to keep it from being overwhelmed.

"It's the desire to maintain it as a living culture, an ongoing, evolving culture," Sanborn said.

She spoke as one who had lived away. A smart kid, valedictorian when she graduated at sixteen, she went to university in the Lower Mainland, but always with the intent of returning to Alert Bay. People there have a keen sense of place, of their environment being part of who they are.

That sense of identity was crucial to Sanborn. She saw no contradiction in buying iPhones and cheering for the Canucks while also eating eulachon grease or tossing the skeleton of the first salmon of the year into the sea as a gesture of gratitude. "Maybe we have Saks Fifth Avenue clothing on now instead of cedar bark robes, but the culture carries on, is still respected," she once told me. It was a loss for all when a brain tumour claimed her at age sixty-two in 2010.

Bill Cranmer only had to walk around Village Island for reminders of how fragile a minority culture can be, though. 'Mimkwamlis has been uninhabited since the early 1960s, when the Department of Indian Affairs herded the residents to Alert Bay.

The area may be beautiful, but it was remarkably short of signs of human life on this day. Harbour porpoises and eagles escorted the boat in which Cranmer travelled. A great blue heron perched on a rock. Marbled murrelets and black turnstones darted by. An abandoned fishboat rotted on a wild shore. The surviving portion of a dock, sitting on thick pilings, had become a moss-covered island. Not far away, on Turnour Island, ancient pictographs—images of the sun, three sailing ships, a stagecoach—faded into the cliffs.

In 2013, all 113 pieces on display at the U'mista Cultural Centre suffered smoke damage after children set off a marine flare, accidentally starting a fire under the building. It would take months to restore twenty-two masks that were water-logged when the sprinklers went off. The good news is that they didn't actually get burned.

It's hard to overstate what that loss would have meant, for U'mista is not—and this is said with all respect to other institutions—just another local museum, the potlatch display not just another collection.

"It's priceless," Bill Cranmer said.

"It represents all the suffering our old people went through in the potlatch prohibition, the fight they went through to keep our history alive."

don catterall

BOB REMINGTON DIDN'T trust Don Catterall when he spotted him standing in front of the James Bay plaza. He figured the friendliness was an act, a way to lure some spare change into the upturned cap.

"When I first saw him, all the biases of my comfortable life came out," Remington said. Then he discovered, as did the rest of the neighbourhood, that the act was real, that the homeless man genuinely cared about the people who streamed past his sidewalk post each day.

"I bet Don knew, by name, a thousand people in James Bay," Doug Snowsell says. A pastor, Snowsell presided over an informal memorial for Catterall outside the plaza, on Simcoe Street, on an April morning in 2017.

Memorial services for homeless people are often insular affairs, a matter of one member of the street community being eulogized by others. A smattering of the latter were among the seventy people who gathered at this one, but the crowd was a cross-section of James Bay—young parents with babies, merchants, Gore-Texed retirees (and a few of their dogs)—all professing a real sense of loss. Starbucks brought out coffee, for free; the people who work there liked the fifty-two-year-old Catterall, too.

The neighbours took turns telling stories of how they took care of him and he looked out for them. Plenty had hired him to do work around their homes. One woman brought him a hot meal pretty much every day. When the weather turned cold and Don fell ill that winter, someone in the neighbourhood said, "Come stay in my spare room." That's where they found Don when he died.

It was easy to see how much he had touched people in James Bay over the previous couple of years. What's harder to explain is how he got there.

Don grew up around the Saanich Peninsula, a happy kid who knew every inch of Cordova Bay beach. He attended Cordova Bay, Royal Oak, and Parkland schools, though it didn't come easily to him.

"One day he said to me, 'Dad, I don't like going to school anymore,'" his father, Ken, recalled. So instead of graduating, Don went into construction with his dad, who taught him how to use heavy equipment—bulldozers, crushers, that sort of thing.

Exactly why or when things went sideways is hard to say. Don was maybe forty when he gave up construction in favour of odd-jobbing. He would disappear for long stretches.

Mental health? Yes, he ended up in the psychiatric ward a decade ago during one of his disappearances, but those in James Bay saw no outward indications of mental illness. Substance abuse? The autopsy showed fentanyl, but some people at the service said he wasn't a user; some suspected that Don, his health declining, had been given a pill to make him feel better. Poverty? He worked like a demon, harder than people with steady jobs, but money didn't mean much to him. Homeless? Yes, but he could have lived with his parents had he wanted to. Instead, he just dropped out of sight altogether in 2013.

His family searched for him and took out newspaper ads, to no avail. Ken would come down from Parksville, where he lived, and scour the streets. Other relatives looked, too. Nobody thought to look by the planter on the sidewalk in front of the James Bay Starbucks, though.

Family members at least got to hear Don remembered fondly at the memorial. "When I broke my arm, he was more concerned about my health than I was about his health," one man said. Words like *respectful*, *polite*, and *genuine* were repeated.

"He seemed as concerned for everybody in the neighbourhood as they were about him," Remington said. Bad knees hampered Don's ability to get a job, to get on top of life, but "he never asked anybody to feel sorry for him."

Snowsell, who had met Don two and a half years before, when the latter was living under a bridge in Beacon Hill Park, called him "one of the most spiritual people I've met—not religious, but spiritual."

Joan Athey recalled Don knocking on the door of her home, asking her for ten dollars so that he could buy a new inhaler for his asthma. She gave him the money but was taken aback by the uncharacteristic request. The next week he apologized to her for having to ask. Now Athey wonders what kind of a society reduces an asthmatic man to begging for money for a puffer. It angers her that the help Don needed—with housing, finances, his health—was so hard to get. "I thought this was a preventable death."

Homeless people get tossed around like a political football during election campaigns, are often treated less as human beings than as a problem to be solved. In James Bay, people didn't see "the homeless." They saw Don.

light of my life

ON HIS RARE forays ashore, Larry Douglas goes crazy seeing people in public washrooms who leave the taps running, letting all that precious water pour straight down the drain.

"I just go nuts," he says on this day in 2003. "Water is gold."

Just one of the lessons learned in a quarter century spent in BC's lighthouses, where conservation becomes second nature.

Some people probably think Larry is nuts anyway, spending all that time alone in the middle of nowhere, but the fifty-seven-year-old isn't really alone. He has all the company he needs in his wife, Avril.

And therein lies the key to their choice to spend their adult lives far, far away from grocery stores, Petro-Cans, friends, offices, 7-Elevens, and all the other trappings of normal existence. "We wanted to be together all the time," shrugs Larry, sitting in the cozy kitchen of their Entrance Island home.

Stick many couples on an isolated outpost and somebody would come off in handcuffs. Not Larry and Avril. After twenty-five years on the lights together, they still moon around like newlyweds. Theirs is a love story—one that seems destined to outlast the lighthouse life they cherish.

Alas for the Douglases, and for the boaters and aviators who value the work they do, some in Ottawa feel Canada's remaining staffed lighthouses have too much to do with romance and too little to do with service.

In December 2002, federal Auditor General Sheila Fraser complained about the $72 million that Canada has spent staffing fifty lighthouses, including twenty-seven in BC, since 1998. "It is now accepted that staffed light stations are not necessary for maritime safety and navigation," she wrote.

Not the sort of thing they like to hear on Entrance Island, which has had a light since 1875, but barely survived destaffing in 1998. Sixteen of BC's forty-three lights no longer have a human presence.

The Douglases bristle at the suggestion that their work isn't needed. People want to deal with people, not just machines, particularly when it comes to personal safety. Mariners trust the keepers. The Entrance Island light gets regular calls from airlines asking about visibility and weather for planes taking off and landing in Nanaimo. "They wouldn't fly a lot of times if they couldn't get hold of us out here," says Larry.

And don't forget the Boxing Day storm of a few years back, when waves pushing two metres threw a log into the path of a lone kayaker, dunking him in the frigid waters near Entrance Island. He couldn't get back in the kayak and was left clinging to its hull. The Douglases wrestled the lighthouse boat into the water and Larry and son Robert set off to the rescue. Big Robert one-handed the weakened kayaker out of the chuck. Let's see an automated foghorn try that.

Barren, schoolyard-sized Entrance Island certainly doesn't look like a battleground. It's actually pretty civilized by light-house standards, just a few minutes by boat—weather permitting—from Gabriola Island. Dotted around its windswept three acres are the light tower, a boathouse, an engine room, a cistern building, a house for Larry and Avril and another for Robert, the assistant keeper and only other resident— unless you count the sea lions.

Larry tried counting the sea lions in May and stopped at four hundred. They began showing up about seven years ago, appearing with the warm weather, then heading back to California after a couple of months. Good thing their stay is short—the roaring, barking din is deafening, and it doesn't take much to set them off. "They're like watchdogs."

A few days ago, Larry notes, a pod of passing killer whales scared the sea lions high up on the rocks. That's where one of them died last year. It was too big to move and lay there until washed away by a storm. Got pretty ripe, too. Yucch.

Larry and Avril talk about the island's wildlife the way other people talk about their neighbours. They laugh at the nervous seals that fled to the far end of the island when those rowdy sea lions moved in. A killdeer nesting outside is treated like a family friend. "She's a great little bird," he says. They're waiting for her four eggs to hatch.

A couple of pairs of oystercatchers are also under watch. The Douglases try to keep the ground-nesting birds safe. "We're not allowed to have cats," notes Avril. Once, a snowy owl stopped by for three days. It tore the seagulls to shreds.

Other birds abound. "Sometimes you see eagles sitting all over the lawn," says Avril. "They look like chickens." As she speaks, a turkey vulture hangs in the wind outside the kitchen window.

The kitchen is comfy as can be. The tablecloth bears a lighthouse motif, as do the napkins. The wall calendar bears a picture of a lighthouse. Framed lighthouse photos hang on the wall. You get the idea. "We like it to be warm and friendly," Avril says.

They have a satellite dish and just got the Internet, but the windows offer a better show: ferries run to Tsawwassen and Horseshoe Bay, and a steady traffic of freighters, tug-and-tows, sailboats, prawn-fishing boats, and kayaks cruises by. On some summer nights, the Douglases can see passengers dancing in passing cruise ships.

Outside, snapdragons, snow-in-summer, valerian, alyssum, and wallflowers grow from a rock garden. The Douglases have put a lot of effort into this place in their dozen years here.

Before that it was the lights at Boat Bluff, Quatsino, Ballenas, Lucy Island, and Langara. Their story began one night when Ladysmith-raised Larry met Scottish-born Avril at a dance in Nanaimo. "We knew at that moment we were going to get married," she says. He provides the echo: "It was love at first sight." They got hitched.

Larry had logged and worked in the mill at Harmac, but it wasn't what they wanted. "It was actually my wife who said, 'What about lighthouses?'" recalls Larry. She had spent time on lights earlier in life. They applied and were accepted.

Their first posting was Langara Point, the Siberia of BC light stations, up at the north end of Haida Gwaii. "When I got to Langara and that ship pulled away, I said, 'What on earth am I doing here?'" Larry says. It was so isolated that they would run outside and wave every time a plane flew overhead.

Adapting wasn't easy, particularly when weather delayed the monthly supply ship. "Once, when we were on Langara, we ran out of groceries," says Larry. "We had six cans of creamed corn between the three of us." Those cans had to serve as dog food, too.

They learned to live with what they had, and to work things out when necessary. "We've never, ever gone to bed mad at each other," says Larry. "Where am I going to go, anyway? Down to the engine room?" Lighthouses test relationships, says Avril. "It will either make or break a marriage." Many break.

Life became easier when the Douglases got close enough to civilization that they could fetch their own supplies. But even going shopping can be hair-raising for a lightkeeper. Larry and Avril still don't know why their fibreglass boat didn't go under when a storm swamped them as they were returning to the Ballenas light one time. "All the groceries were floating around in the boat," says Avril.

These days, they keep a car at a friend's place on Gabriola, and shuttle back and forth in the station's Zodiac-style boat. Once, Avril got all the way back to Entrance Island with a load of shopping, only to find the weather too rough to dock. She chucked the frozen food up to Larry on the island, then turned the boat around and headed for a hotel room ashore.

(That grocery shopping includes the aforementioned water, which comes from shore in four-litre bottles. They collect rain runoff from the roof, but even after filtration it's only good for bathing and cleaning, not drinking.)

It's an existence that can be more than just inconvenient. Three years ago, Avril was diagnosed with cancer. She was operated on successfully, but three days later had a pulmonary embolism while recovering in Nanaimo hospital. "If I had been out here, I wouldn't have survived," she says.

After her release, she had to go to Nanaimo for medical treatment twice a week, sometimes by boat, sometimes by helicopter. That was tough, particularly in the stormy winter. "But I'm fine now," she declares. "I'm fit."

That wasn't her first reminder of how remote a lighthouse can be in a medical emergency. While on her own at the Quatsino light—Larry was off in a boat—she fell and shattered her knee. A helicopter flew in to get her but was turned back by bad weather on the return leg to hospital. Everyone—the Douglases, the paramedic, the pilot—had to spend the night at the lighthouse.

Even on a station as close to urban life as Entrance Island, there isn't much human contact. "It might be six weeks before we go grocery shopping sometimes," says Larry. "We won't see anybody in that time."

A hovercraft from Vancouver drops diesel for the generators, thirteen thousand litres at a time, but social calls are few. "You don't get a lot of visitors here," says Avril. "It's a hard island to get on to."

What does she miss from the outside world? "Nothing. Over the years, you adjust to what you've got, what you can do." She knits a lot—socks with a diamond pattern are a favourite. She's a voracious reader, dropping three or four hundred dollars on every trip to Bolen Books in Victoria. Mention the Scottish butcher shop in Brentwood Bay and her eyes light up. Ayrshire ham, black pudding. Yummy.

For Larry, it's ice cream. "When I get out here, I want a banana split. But when I get to town, I don't want one anymore." He misses having a classic car—maybe a Corvette—on which to work. "That's probably my only regret."

In Nanaimo one day, he bought a raffle ticket for a Mustang. "The ticket seller said, 'We'll deliver it if you win.' I said, 'No, you won't.'"

Regular maintenance keeps him busy: painting and washing the buildings, cleaning the solar-powered light, servicing the generators, mowing that great big lawn. A lightkeeper needs to know a bit about carpentry, plumbing, electricity. "It's surprising. You'd think you would have time on your hands, but you don't really." Fine by him. "I can't stand being idle."

The Douglases know they have, at best, a few more years before they have to leave the lighthouse life. Even if the government doesn't pull the plug, retirement isn't far away. They'll buy a house then, maybe in Scotland. Until then, they'll make the most of the moments they have.

"I've loved every minute of it," says Avril.

EPILOGUE

OTTAWA'S 2003 ATTEMPT to remove staff from lighthouses eventually foundered. The Harper Conservatives took one last run at the idea in 2009 but, with a federal election pending and a fresh-off-the-press Senate committee report defending the need for lightkeepers, backed off in 2011.

"Because of their presence at isolated and critical points along Canada's coasts, lightkeepers perform a variety of safety-related functions and services that are vitally important to mariners and aviators," the Senate report read.

In 2014, an Entrance Island lightkeeper raced to the rescue of nine people after their boat overturned one nautical mile to the north.

Larry and Avril Douglas stayed on Entrance Island until 2008. They didn't want to go, but Larry hurt his back when a piece of ground at the edge of the island gave way one day, and the doctor said he couldn't go back to work.

They moved to Port Alberni, which is where their love story had its final chapter. Avril passed away in 2010.

nathalia buchan

SHE WAS STILL a toddler when her father, Colonel Pyotr Reksting, roused the family in the middle of the Siberian night. "The Bolsheviks are at the next town. They've shot everyone. You have five minutes to pack."

And so began a journey that ended in Victoria in December 2010 when Nathalia Buchan died at one hundred years of age.

One of her earliest memories was of crossing frozen Lake Baikal by train. They switched to horse and carriage to cross the Chinese border, coming to rest in Harbin, Manchuria.

In 1929, with Japan muscling up to Manchuria, nineteen-year-old Nathalia fled again, this time alone, to Shanghai. Nathalia was educated by now, spoke seven languages, had attended the University of Peking. She became manager at DD's, a famed Shanghai nightclub.

One day a young Scot walked into the club. Having run away from school to fly biplanes in the First World War, Bill Buchan had landed in China after Lady Nancy Astor hooked him up with a telephone company undertaking a construction project in the Far East. He entered DD's in a foul mood, was rude to the staff. "My mother, in the most polite way, put him in his place," says their son, David Buchan.

Bill liked that. Still, it was two years before he contacted Nathalia, sending her two huge opera baskets of flowers, piled taller than a man, when she was sick. It wasn't until Remembrance Day 1941 that they married, reasoning that she would be better with a British passport when the Japanese invaded Shanghai's International Settlement, which they did less than a month later, the day after Pearl Harbor was attacked. "I will never let you down," he promised her.

Having been born in Russia, which, unlike Britain, was not at war with Japan, Nathalia was given the option of freedom, but chose to follow her husband into the Lunghua internment camp—the one depicted in the movie *Empire of the Sun*. "I will not be parted from the man I love," she said.

They remained in Lunghua until 1946, after the war, their survival due in no small part to the repeated kindness of the camp commandant, Captain Tomohiko Hayashi, a brave man who was known to risk his own well-being by inserting himself between the prisoners and a faction of cruel guards who were beyond his control. On one occasion, Hayashi sent Nathalia, sick with rheumatic fever, to hospital in Shanghai in his car, giving her enough money for medicine, lunch for herself and her guards, and a cake to bring back to Bill. (In 2013, dismayed by the way Hayashi was portrayed in *Empire of the Sun*, David persuaded Victoria MP Murray Rankin to rise in the House of Commons to honour "the Japanese Schindler." Watching from the gallery, a tear running down his cheek, was Hayashi's seventy-seven-year-old son, Sadayuki, a former Japanese ambassador to Britain.)

Despite Hayashi's kindness, Nathalia was in rough shape, weighing just seventy-eight pounds, when they were liberated by American troops at the end of the war.

With Shanghai in chaos and China locked in a communist-nationalist struggle, the Buchans alighted in Bangkok. Bill sold newsprint from BC before building up a tobacco business.

One day in 1946 there was a knock on the door. There, the story goes, stood two Vietnamese leaders—Ho Chi Minh and Vo Nguyen Giap—looking to buy arms with which to fight French occupation. The two men later became household names worldwide, synonymous with the struggle first against the French, then the US and South Vietnam, but at this point their campaign was just getting going.

"The Russians said you could help us," they told Bill.

Bill left for Czechoslovakia to broker the deal, but not before stopping at the British embassy to pick up a pistol for Nathalia; he didn't want to leave her defenceless in lawless Bangkok. "We're fresh out of pistols," said a Peter Lorre look-alike at the embassy, "but I have something better." He produced a Thompson submachine gun, the kind gangsters used to wield in the movies. Every evening, Nathalia, still half-blind and emaciated from wartime malnutrition, would hobble onto the veranda on her crutches, place a pillow between the Tommy gun and her shoulder, and rip off a couple of bursts to keep the bandits at bay.

The Buchans built up the tobacco business but lost everything when it was nationalized by the Thai government. So they started anew, growing another prosperous trading company after moving to Hong Kong in 1952. It was there that David was born—and that his father died in 1958. Nathalia ran the business alone—a European speaking Chinese dialect in a man's world—until she sold it in 1962 after falling ill.

They had tickets to England, but someone convinced her Canada would be a better place to raise her son. They sailed—David, Nathalia, her mother—on the P&O liner *Arcadia*, a three-and-a-half-week voyage. Vancouver was cold and rainy, but the clouds parted when they visited Victoria. "A sign from God. We will settle here," Nathalia said.

And so they did. David took root in Victoria, became a manager in the provincial government. Nathalia never remarried. "I loved your father so much that I could never bear the thought of marrying anyone else," she told her son.

Canada gave Nathalia a quiet life, or at least quieter than the one in Asia. (There is a story of how she helped raise the actor Yul Brynner after he befriended her cousin in Shanghai. "He was literally living on the streets and stealing motorcycles, stuff like that," David says.) In Victoria, she was part of a small community of Europeans who drifted to the BC capital from Asia after the war. (Princess Peggy Abkhazi, of Abkhazi Garden fame, was Nathalia's across-the-road neighbour in the Lunghua internment camp.)

Nathalia lived in Victoria's Glengarry Hospital for her last couple of years, had dementia at the end. But perhaps you saw her before that, when she was still in her mid-nineties, poking down Oak Bay Avenue with her walker. Perhaps you looked right through her, not knowing she was this courageous, pious, compassionate, fiercely intelligent woman inching toward the end of a hundred-year journey.

the pender island
woodchoppers

JANE McINTOSH WAS having a crappy couple of weeks. It was two years since her husband had died of cancer. Her boss was seriously ill. The man who was to carve a memorial pole for her husband's ashes died before the work could be done. Her best friend's husband had a heart attack.

The thing is, every time something went wrong, David Howe would call with good news.

I just chopped another cord of wood for you, he would say. Or maybe he'd tell her that another Pender Island family had given her a downed tree.

You see, Jane was about to volunteer on a hospital ship in Africa for two years, and David and his axe were helping pay her way there.

Jane first: She and her husband, John, had wanted to continue their volunteer work with the Mennonite Central Committee, but John died three months after they moved to Pender from Ontario in 2008. Signing on with Mercy Ships, a Christian charity with its Canadian headquarters in Victoria, seemed the right thing to do. "It was unfinished business for me," the fifty-six-year-old mother of three grown daughters said, just before heading off, the day after Boxing Day in 2010. She was looking forward to spending two years living with 450 others on a converted Dutch ferry—bunk beds and dorms, just like summer camp—where it would be her job to sterilize medical instruments. One problem, though: her flights, room and board, and other expenses would cost her $1,200 a month, which is where David Howe came in.

At the time, David was a sixty-six-year-old investment banker. He grew up on the Saanich Peninsula before a business career took him to the US, Mexico, and Switzerland. He was in London, England, when he got in touch with his boyhood sweetheart, Ina Timmer, who had stayed in his heart even though they hadn't spoken in twenty-seven years.

How are you, he asked. Divorced, she replied. "Let me put you on hold a moment," he said, and quickly got his secretary to book him a flight to Victoria. By 2010 David and Ina had been married eighteen years and had lived on Pender for seven.

He's big on socially responsible development, is an idealist, believes in the concept of service; around 2006, he began looking for a way to turn his beliefs into action on Pender.

"One thing I know how to do is swing an axe," said David, who, at a strapping six foot two, looks more like a lumberjack than a banker. So he began chopping his neighbours' wood. Didn't matter if those neighbours were rich or poor, he always refused payment for doing so—it was that service-to-others thing—until he met Jane McIntosh.

Jane asked him to split some fallen trees on her property, explaining that she wanted to sell the wood to finance her Mercy Ships effort. Okay, said David, and anybody else who wants to pay for my wood-splitting can send their money to the same place.

Word spread around the island. George and Penny Finkbeiner said they would donate a fallen two-hundred-year-old fir on their property. Another guy said he would deliver the split wood and pick up cheques for Jane. Some simply sent cheques to Mercy Ships in her name. By the time she left, seven or eight people were involved in raising cordwood cash. David had chopped maybe twenty cords of wood for Jane by then. "When I'm on the island, I try to do about a cord a day, seven days a week," he said. Not that big a deal, he added, not when Jane was giving up two years of her life.

Funny thing is, the woodchopping didn't stop after she left. In fact, the effort kept growing: by the time Jane got back, two years later, the Greenangels Foundation had been born. About thirty-five islanders, including a core of up to a dozen choppers, were involved in the ongoing effort, bucking up, splitting, and selling. A couple of backhoe operators volunteered to pull timber from the bush. Other volunteers ferried over with full pickup trucks from Mayne Island, then pitched in with the chopping on Pender. Ina Timmer stacked wood and kept the books straight.

Other islanders both donated and bought the wood. Former Alberta cabinet minister Jim Dinning gave ten cords from his land. Another new arrival from Alberta surrendered the fallen fir and arbutus from his twenty-five-acre property, then bought back the split arbutus for $4,000—twice the going rate.

By late 2016 the choppers, almost all of them retirees, had raised about $100,000, one cord at a time. About $15,000 went to Mercy Ships, but most of the projects were local. They raised $13,000 for a generator at the community hall, an emergency power supply for the island. There was money for a gardening project at the school. When a six-month-old baby needed a kidney transplant, they helped the family get to Edmonton. Ditto when someone needed an eye operation. On and on it went: the food bank, a beach cleanup, trail-building, lacrosse, Habitat for Humanity, parks, kids' summer programs, the Pender bus . . .

They forged new relationships and tightened old ones. David, who sat on the regional district board, would stop on the Saanich Peninsula on his way to meetings in Victoria to deliver to the Tsawout First Nation a truckload of cedar from Pender (their traditional territory) for ceremonial burning.

Time caught up with the woodchoppers eventually. By November 2016, with most of the axemen in their seventies, the business of cutting and hauling cordwood had become a bit much. They dissolved their foundation.

When Jane heard the choppers were hanging it up, she wrote a letter of gratitude detailing what their contribution had meant in Africa. Not only did they fund her, but they paid to support and train two men from Sierra Leone who continued to work on the hospital ship. They funded a woman who developed equipment that sterilizes medical instruments in places with poor water and electrical supplies. Another guy they helped works with an eye surgery charity. After George Finkbeiner (nicknamed Navajo Joe for his ability to scout out trees to cut) died in 2013, a memorial Kiva micro-lending account was set up that made hundreds of loans to entrepreneurs in thirty-six countries. That then spun into support for the Victoria-based African Community Project's initiative to promote sustainable forests through the planting of millions of seeds.

"You did this," Jane wrote to the Pender Island choppers.

Yes, they did. Behold the power of a grey-hair with an axe.

pat carney

PAT CARNEY IS the exception. One of the rules I laid out for myself when deciding who to include in this book was No Politicians Allowed. And nobody famous. They get enough ink and don't need any more. So, by rights, Carney doesn't belong.

Except Carney isn't really a politician, at least not anymore. Today she's the woman who sells you tickets at the Canada Day lamb barbecue on Saturna Island. And if she decides you haven't bought enough she sells you some more, whether you want them or not. She has that effect on people. It's hard to say no.

I mentioned this to Priscilla Ewbank—another of the women who keep Saturna afloat—one day. "Whenever I talk to Pat Carney," I said, "there comes a point in the conversation where she says, 'Now, Jack, here is what you *must do.*' Then I do what she says, because it's not like she's giving me a choice."

To which Ewbank, a formidably principled presence who shrinks from no one—not Nixon during Vietnam, not Harper during the pipeline debate—admitted that she, too, has bent before Carney's ineluctable edicts. ("Now, Priscilla, here is what you *must do.*")

No one begrudges this because when Carney uses her voice, it's usually on behalf of the voiceless. Also, as a rare female federal cabinet minister in the 1980s, Carney had to be clear and assertive or risk getting drowned out by an all-male chorus.

Carney will be best remembered as the Mulroney-era trade minister during the birth of the US-Canada free trade agreement. Less well documented has been her continuing passion for BC's coastal communities, isolated outposts often ignored by politicians preoccupied with the problems of more populous, vote-rich areas.

It's not surprising that Carney is attracted to issues found at the end of dirt roads. Although elected as an MP from Vancouver, she has lived much of her life at the edges. She was born in China in 1935 to a Canadian father who had grown restless after serving in the First World War and a mother who fell for him while sailing from Vancouver to marry a cousin in Hong Kong. Dora Sanders got off the *Empress of Russia* with Jim Carney in Shanghai and wed him instead.

Chased back to Canada by war, the Carneys eventually ended up on a ranch in the Kootenays. After studying economics at the University of British Columbia, Pat went on to become a business columnist for *The Vancouver Sun*, which is how she got to know the coastal fishing and forestry towns from Alaska south. She then ran her own economic consulting company in the Far North.

Recruited, reluctantly, to run for the Progressive Conservatives, she served as a member of parliament from 1980 to 1988—a time when, as fellow Tory senator Hugh Segal later put it in a tribute, "a paternalistic, old boys, golf club, male Ottawa culture deeply resisted strong, competent and take-no-nonsense women."

In 1990 came an appointment to the Senate, where she sat until her early retirement at age seventy-two in 2008. The *Sun*'s Barbara Yaffe once wrote that Carney did the impossible: "She made the Senate look as if it was inhabited by live human beings preoccupied by the affairs of state."

Carney became known as the self-appointed Defender of the Coast.

A fight to keep a fuel dock in Kyuquot? There was Carney. Navigational aids for mariners? There she was again, battling the Ottawa bureaucracy. She fought to match construction of a Haida Gwaii dock to the fishing season, to advocate for Indigenous women who would otherwise be ignored. "I was constantly dealing with sunken ships, crab issues, tidewater issues, unemployment insurance issues in communities where there was no unemployment office," she says.

The placement of fish farms, the exodus of families, the abandonment of forestry—it all got her going, as did the shift to urban centres. "The bulk of BC's wealth comes from our resources," she once said. "The rest of it comes from taking in each other's laundry." Closing the schools and other services that allow people to remain in small towns cuts access to the source of the province's wealth, forces people to move to the cities. "That's a Third World concept . . . not everyone can live from Nanaimo down."

Her last victory before retiring from the Senate was passage of the Heritage Lighthouse Protection Act. It took seven tries, but she finally pushed through legislation that, in essence, prevents the Department of Fisheries and Oceans from tearing down, burning down, or neglecting to death old light stations (all of which have happened) before first seeing if anyone wants to take responsibility for them. She got to mark that win by—after doing a stint at the market at the

Saturna recycling centre, where she was selling garden plants on behalf of her church—heading down to an open house at the East Point lighthouse, a lonely, windswept, red-roofed building looking down on the shore, where orcas come to rub against the rocks.

As a result of Carney's bill, volunteers were able to work with Parks Canada and regional government to transform the lighthouse's fog alarm building into a community asset known as the Saturna Heritage Centre. Go there today and some cheerful retiree will tell you all about the island's brush with Spanish exploration, the Pig War, or the story of Moby Doll. (The latter was a whale whose tale is credited with changing man's relationship with previously feared orcas: In 1964 a Vancouver Aquarium team set up a harpoon on the East Point cliffs, their goal being to kill a passing killer whale for use as a full-scale model for a sculpture in the aquarium's lobby. After harpooning but only wounding an orca, whose shrill cries could be heard one hundred metres away as it thrashed and struggled to free itself for the next two hours, its captors took it for study in Vancouver, where the public grew to adore it. The whole story is told in Mark Leiren-Young's award-winning book *The Killer Whale Who Changed the World*.)

That the Saturna centre is volunteer-driven is no surprise. There is an automatic expectation that people on the Gulf Islands, and on the isolated outposts of the coast, will pitch in and take on those tasks that urbanites leave to government, Carney says. "I think the people who live in small towns have a sense of community that you don't get in the big cities. They have to rely on themselves and each other."

An example of that is Saturna's legendary annual Canada Day barbecue, when the whole island pulls together and raises enough money in one day to pay for all those services

Victorians expect to be provided by government. Each July 1, up to two thousand people flock (as it were) to the lamb barbecue, arriving by boat (Winter Cove looks like the staging area for the Miracle of Dunkirk) or ferry (Saturna residents use their own cars to shuttle foot passengers to the barbecue site for free). The barbecue—twenty-seven lamb carcasses Stonehenged around an open wood fire—usually sells out, 1,200 lamb dinners netting the community club something like twenty thousand dollars. That pays for the medical centre, the cemetery, the community hall, the library underneath St. Christopher's church, the recycling program, the Christmas party, and all the other stuff run by the Saturna Community Club, which appears to be the closest thing the island has to municipal government.

It's left to volunteers—150 of them on an island with just 350 full-time residents—to make the barbecue work. And that's not counting those who volunteer at the Canada Day event for other groups. The Oystercatchers softball team sells burgers. The 50-50 draw funds yoga and pickleball at the rec centre. The school PAC sells pop and water (school enrolment was up to five children last year, plus ten in the preschool program, a big jump). The firefighters do the dunk tank, sending the proceeds to burn units in Victoria and Vancouver.

The event has been held every year since 1950, when Jim and Lorraine Campbell started the Dominion Day tradition as a school picnic on their sheep farm. The 2016 barbecue, the sixty-seventh, was the first without the couple, who were described as the backbone of Saturna. Jim died November 29, 2015, at age ninety-seven. Lorraine, his wife of more than seventy years, followed him in February at ninety-four. Daughter Jacques Campbell—it's pronounced "Jackie"—runs the farm now, along with the abattoir where those twenty-seven lambs get sent to the Big Pasture in the Sky.

Admission is free, the beer is cold, there are games for the kids, and even the adults get to engage in tugs-of-war, nail-driving contests, and sack races (though—alas—it is no longer deemed appropriate to hold the event in which two couples, chosen from the crowd at random, race to catch and diaper a pig). It's all very wholesome, in an *Anne-of-Green-Gables-meets-The-Beachcombers* kind of way.

The flavour is reflected in Carney's bestselling collection of short stories, *On Island: Life Among the Coast Dwellers*. This is how she has reinvented herself in her eighties, as a writer of fiction. The reaction from coastal BC has been rewarding, she says. "Everybody identifies with the characters. People recognize them as authentic."

It's a long way from Ottawa, a long way from being a politician.

millennium bomber

IT WAS THE evening of December 14, 1999, when Ahmed Ressam drove off the ferry from Victoria on his way to blowing up Los Angeles International Airport.

Thank God that Diana Dean—a sweet-natured, middle-aged customs inspector in Port Angeles, Washington—was there to catch him, something Canadian authorities had failed to do.

Dean was one of five US Customs inspectors screening traffic coming off the MV *Coho*, the marine link between Victoria and its just-visible-across-the-strait neighbour, that night. It was a very light load, just twenty vehicles. "Ressam's was the last car off the ferry," she recalled.

Ressam pulled up in a rented Chrysler with BC plates, but produced a driver's licence identifying him as Benni Noris of Montreal.

Where are you going, Dean asked. "Sattle" is what his reply sounded like.

What for? "Visit." He was nervous, fidgeting, rummaging around on the console for who knows what.

Dean decided to do a secondary search, but first gave him a customs declaration form, just to keep his hands busy as much as anything else.

Where was he staying in Seattle?

"Hotel."

Dean called over fellow inspector Mark Johnson, who had been to Montreal, to question the driver. When Johnson asked for ID, the driver handed over his Costco card. Johnson took the man to a table to check his pockets.

Another inspector popped the trunk and pulled the cover off the spare-tire well. Tucked away where the wheel should have been were plastic bags of white powder, olive jars full of liquid, and a couple of ibuprofen bottles.

Bingo.

Ressam broke free and took off. Inspectors gave chase, but Ressam had a head start. "He ran a good four or five blocks," Dean said. Ressam tried to force his way into a car that was stopped for a red light, but the driver locked her door and hit the gas, throwing him off balance. The customs inspectors jumped him. Police hauled him away.

Johnson and Dean began testing the white powder for various drugs. "We didn't know what it was."

They were joined by Dean's husband, Tony, who had come to the ferry terminal to meet her. That's when they realized what else was in the trunk: four homemade electrical timers. Tony blurted out a couple of words that Diana won't repeat.

That's when the truth sunk in. The man's name wasn't Noris. The powder wasn't drugs. "I knew exactly what we had," Dean said. "My heart went right down to my toes."

After that, all the acronyms poured in: the FBI, the ATF. Ressam was taken away, as were the contents of the trunk, which turned out to be bomb-making ingredients. "It's a good thing we didn't test the ibuprofen bottles," says Dean. They contained the detonator, a substance so sensitive that it could have sparked an explosion had they removed the bottle caps.

It turns out Ressam was on his way to blowing up a passenger terminal in Los Angeles on January 1, 2000. He and another Algerian had cooked up the bomb ingredients in a Vancouver motel. He was free despite being the subject of an immigration warrant and theft charges—and the Canadian Security Intelligence Service's warning that he had gone to Afghanistan for terrorist training.

In 2001, Ressam, who became known as the Millennium Bomber, was convicted of nine counts in relation to the bomb plot. Facing up to 130 years in prison, he began to co-operate with authorities, reportedly telling them that cells of Al-Qaeda terrorists were in the US—information included in a report titled *Bin Laden Determined to Strike in US* that was passed to President George W. Bush just a month before the 9/11 terrorist attacks. Ressam was eventually sentenced to thirty-seven years in prison.

That episode didn't mark the first time we have given our southern neighbours reason to be wary about the border, of course. BC has long been a smugglers' paradise. Vancouver Island, with its long stretches of sparsely populated coastline, has a particularly proud history of illegal activity, everything from dope going south to ships backed with Fujianese migrants trying to slip into our remoter reaches unnoticed.

It goes back more than a century. A *Times Colonist* piece written by Andrei Bondoreff detailed the cross-border trade that flourished in the 1890s, when Victoria-based white smugglers were paid twenty to twenty-five dollars a head to spirit Chinese migrants into Washington State. Opium flowed south, too, while cheap cigarettes came north. So did bootleg liquor sold straight from American schooners to reserves during the days when the law barred Indigenous people from buying alcohol.

After the US brought in Prohibition in 1920, the booze flowed south. Rum-runners like Johnny Schnarr, who made four hundred trips from Victoria to the US, some in fast boats powered by aircraft engines, became minor legends. Cadboro Bay's Smugglers' Cove Pub comes by its name honestly (or dishonestly).

Later the trade was in drugs, the common image in the 1990s and 2000s being small boats zipping south across the strait—less than twenty kilometres wide in places—with hockey bags stuffed with BC Bud. ("It's always hockey bags," the Victoria-raised cop in charge of the Olympic Peninsula's narcotics squad once told me. "I could outfit the Canucks.")

Sometimes the stories were almost comical. In 2006, undercover officers posing as anglers had to help smugglers wrestle their Ecstasy-packed craft—a twenty-four-footer named *Just Chillin'*—onto a too-small trailer that the Keystone Krooks had parked at a boat launch just outside Port Angeles. Then they busted them.

Sometimes the amounts are mind-boggling: in 2001, US authorities seized an incredible 2.5 tonnes of Colombian cocaine valued at $300 million from a Victoria man's tuna boat just before it turned toward the Strait of Juan de Fuca, bound for Vancouver Island.

That was just months before 9/11, and nothing has been the same since. The US border patrol has increased its northern presence greatly, employing some mind-boggling technology. One story stands out: A border patrol agent stationed with a radioactivity-sniffing device on the highway near Bellingham chased down a car that sped by at more than 110 kilometres an hour. It turned out the car was carrying not a nuclear bomb but a cat that had just received radiological treatment. Pause to consider that:

they can now detect a radioactive cat doing 110 kilometres an hour.

It's easy to make fun of that, or at least to grow resentful of the security measures that have made crossing the border a more arduous process. Travellers who prior to 9/11 would slip over to the US with nothing more than a driver's licence or birth certificate must now carry a passport. There are cameras, fences, ion scanners. Airline passengers must not only show up for international flights hours early but also submit to being patted down in a way that should be followed by a cigarette and a marriage proposal. When this happens in leafy, peaceful Victoria, it's easy to roll your eyes and smirk at what seems like overkill—until you remember Ahmed Ressam and Diana Dean, the poster child for vigilance.

Dean retired and moved away from Port Angeles several years ago. I still remember a conversation we had in 2003, though.

She came across as pleasant and open—and still somewhat awed by the enormity of her discovery. "It brought home to us that we might just be a sleepy little town on the peninsula, but terrorists can show up anywhere," she said.

The vast majority of travellers, 99.7 percent, are exactly what they say they are, she said. Customs inspectors look for those who seem out of place. "It's just the one that doesn't fit." In Ressam's case, he was agitated, uncommunicative. "He was very nervous."

Did Dean ever think of the consequences of not catching Ressam?

"Oh, sure. I thank God every day that we stopped him and found what he had."

chez monique

THE HIKERS STAGGER down the West Coast Trail, fifty pounds of sodden gear in their backpacks, one hundred pounds of sand in their boots, a ton of misery in their hearts.

And then, like an oasis in the desert, it appears: Chez Monique, the world's least likely, most appreciated store and restaurant.

It's nothing fancy to look at: Plastic and tarps wrapped around a frame of driftwood logs and rough timber. A handful of tables and chairs scattered at the edge of the beach.

But as they say in business: location, location, location.

Chez Monique hugs the coast just south of Carmanah Point, halfway down the seventy-five-kilometre trail, three days away from civilization for the five thousand or so people who tromp through each year. It's that isolation that allows it to operate beyond the reach of officialdom: no regulation, no business licence, no building permits, no health inspections, no zoning, no nothing except the most delicious cheeseburger ever and a helping hand for those who need one.

It was also the centre of the universe for Monique and Peter Knighton, the couple whose lives were centred there, right up until Monique's death on New Year's Eve, 2017, and Peter's just five months after that. Both were seventy-eight.

I first stumbled across the couple while hiking the trail in 2001. I returned a year later with photographer Debra Brash, boating up with Port Renfrew's Pete Hovey.

We got there just in time for rush hour, fifteen hikers having converged from both directions. They included a bunch from Oregon, a couple of occupational therapists from Kingston, Ontario, a pair of disgustingly healthy and attractive hospital doctors from Sweden.

No shirt, no shoes, no service? Get real. This is the wilderness. Boots were pulled off for blister repair. Shirts got peeled away, revealing red marks where backpack straps had dug into shoulders.

"We've been singing Jimmy Buffett's 'Cheeseburger in Paradise' for the last seven miles," said Jay Bollinger, a muscular young Coloradan who had just arrived at Monique's with three buddies.

Ooh, the burgers. There wasn't much else on the menu, but nobody was complaining. "This is, oh my god, c'est bon," said Ottawa's Betty Organ, gushing in both official languages after her first bite.

A brief dispute ensued over whether Monique's offered the most mouth-watering burger in the world, or whether that was just the hunger-inducing trail talking.

"It's at least number 2," said American Jeremy Hakes.

"I'd say it's number 1," said Bollinger, who appeared ready to propose to his lunch.

But Max Cook remained loyal to a blue cheeseburger back in Seattle. They all ordered a second round, just to make sure.

Other hikers gathered around a table to stock up on those things they had forgotten, run out of, or accidentally dropped down a pit toilet: Advil, film, fresh fruit, bug dope, water tablets, gaiters, chocolate bars, trail mix, liquor. A woman quietly slipped up to Monique to buy some Tampax.

Monique, both outgoing and grandmotherly, took the money and served the food. Peter, less effusive, flipped the burgers, cooked the bacon and eggs, made the hash browns and toast.

Everything here—food, propane for the grill and oven, chests of ice—had to be brought by boat from Port Renfrew. The trip took Peter forty-five minutes to two hours, depending on the weather. It was either that or a seven-kilometre hike up a billy-goat trail to a logging road, followed by a three-hour drive to the bright lights of Duncan or Nanaimo.

There was a garden out back, leading to an outhouse and a dwelling cobbled together in a fashion similar to the restaurant-store. Solar panels fed batteries, but there was really no electricity to speak of. Drinking water came from a creek.

Pretty rustic, but almost urban in comparison to what it looked like when Monique and Peter first moved there on July 1, 1991. "We just had a shelter on the beach with an air mattress and a tarp over our belongings," said Peter. And then it started to rain. They shuddered at the memory.

Peter was born a few kilometres from here, back when there was an Indigenous settlement at Clo-oose. His surname, Knighton, evolved from his grandfather's Nytom, which itself was an anglicized version of an Indigenous name. (When that grandfather got a lifesaving medal for tying a fishing line to himself and swimming through the pounding surf to rescue a pair of shipwrecked sailors, the accompanying certificate identified him as Jimmy Night-Time.)

Peter was only a few years old when he was scooped up and taken away to residential school. He would later tell his long-time friend Hovey that when he finally made it back home, his family, who lived in the old ways, found him different.

There was a divide. "He always thought that he had lost some culture there," says Hovey.

Peter was gone from Vancouver Island for a long time, spending more than twenty years working for a chemical company in the Lower Mainland. It was there in 1984 that he met Montreal-raised Monique, whose French accent made her Irish-Algonquin roots a bit of a surprise.

How they ended up by Carmanah is a little complicated. Peter said it had a lot to do with connecting with his dad, who had trapped, hunted, and fished there. "I just had it in my heart that I wanted to be where he spent so much of his life."

But another factor was that Peter didn't love authority, not after that residential school, not after the way official-dom decided which Indigenous families should be shifted to which reserves. So, at odds with both Ottawa and elements of the Ditidaht band at nearby Nitinat, Peter put some distance between him and them and moved west on that day in 1991. The federal government says the land on which Chez Monique sits is part of the Ditidaht reserve, but Peter only recognized it as being his family's traditional territory. He called it Qwa-ba-diwa, its historical name.

Monique said that when she, Peter, and their ten-year-old daughter, Sandi, moved there, "Peter was making a stand for sovereignty."

They began the stand with almost nothing, just that tarp on the beach. They lived by the laws of nature. Other laws, those of the paved and Starbucked world, were irrelevant.

"The education I got in the city meant nothing," Sandi says. "Life in the city meant nothing."

They didn't come with the intention of doing much other than just living. Chez Monique, which opened in 1993, wasn't really planned. It just gradually emerged as bedraggled hikers turned to the Knightons for help and supplies. "I opened a can of pop and they showed up," said Monique.

When the store came into being back in 1993, the idea was to call it Chez Nytom, but Chez Monique stuck after that name appeared in *Blisters and Bliss*, the guidebook/bible for West Coast Trail hikers. You won't find mention of Monique's in any official Parks Canada literature, as befits its unofficial status.

The absence of licences, certificates, and other signs of regulation is both noticeable and appreciated by hikers. This is the wild west coast, not Yonge and Bloor. The footprint of bureaucratic intervention is not welcome on this beach.

Most of the time Peter and Monique had the place to themselves, their three cats, and one dog. Even during the many years that they lived there year-round, the store was only open during hiking season, May through September. "We have seven months a year where we can be ourselves, with no pressure," said Monique, "and five months a year when we have people."

It wasn't that they were antisocial. Monique was a wonderful raconteur as the hikers slumped around the chairs and tables scattered in the sand, and Hovey says Peter had a great, dry sense of humour. There was a funny story about Peter accidentally puncturing his brand-new inflatable boat with the spine of a rockfish. "Everybody loved the man," Hovey said. "He was a good, straight-shooting guy."

Peter was stubbornly independent, though, neither asking for nor wanting help even as age caught up to him. Hovey would spot him hauling two hundred pounds of ice to his boat, alone, while preparing for one of those supply runs from Port Renfrew to Carmanah. "He was a solitary guy. He wouldn't rely on other people . . . He took his burden on his shoulders."

In any case, Peter and Monique cherished their solitude. She once admitted that the noise of the helicopter that periodically serviced the lighthouse at Carmanah Point drove her "bonkers."

There were non-human visitors—mink, otter, marten, the rare deer. "We've had bears who were fed by hikers and wanted to follow them," Peter said. Orcas and grey whales would put on the occasional show. Their dog once chased a cougar; it slammed into the window of the house, but the glass didn't break.

Isolation had its downfalls, of course. Laundry had to be hauled to town. Monique got choppered out with medical problems once. She said she missed sushi restaurants. He said he missed window shopping.

But mostly it was just peaceful, even in the summer. The hikers would come, fuel up, and leave. And when they were gone, Peter and Monique remained, alone in Eden. On the day Brash, Hovey, and I visited, we feasted on fresh-caught crab. Then, magically, Monique conjured up a rhubarb pie. It was an idyll straight out of *Robinson Crusoe*.

That idyll was hard work, though, even dangerous. When the weather turned, it was a fight just to survive. Hovey noted how often Peter and Monique had been there to save (then cook) the bacon of hikers who had staggered in on the verge of hypothermia. Monique recalled stashing fifty people around the place one night when a storm closed the trail. Twenty-one of them were crammed in a little hut, five guys slept sideways on an air mattress, the greenhouse was full of Germans. Years later, Sandi would recall a childhood spent scampering sure-footed and shoeless through the rocks and logs to bring in blue-lipped, shivering tourists amid storms that would rage and howl for days.

Maintaining a toehold in their wilderness paradise wasn't easy for the Knightons. One of those storms destroyed their boat a few year ago, a crippling blow.

"That place, it's do or die," Sandi says. "It was always such a damned struggle."

Sandi was the first to leave, being well into her teens when she moved to the Lower Mainland, where she pursued a more conventional education.

Peter and Monique hung in for a few more years, but Monique's health concerns changed things. "She really wanted to stay there full-time, but the doctors said it wasn't a good idea," Peter later said.

So they would winter in civilization, returning for the hiking season in May, often with Sandi and other family members in tow.

The couple's last summer at Carmanah, in 2017, was hard. Monique's health was failing, and Peter was almost lost while trying to save their boat in a storm. Recalling that latter tale, the emotion in Sandi's voice rose as she described a hair-raising episode that culminated in her father crashing his boat onto the beach, where she heaved him over her shoulder and hauled him away from the thundering surf. Peter was spent, but not so far gone that he couldn't half-joke as Sandi carried him to safety. "He told me, 'One of these days I'm going to die at home.'"

Later, after they took Peter to hospital, he was found to be suffering from life-threatening sepsis. He wouldn't make it back to Chez Monique until it was time to button things up in September.

Yet in January 2018, just after his wife's death at Victoria General Hospital, Peter was still talking about trying to return to open Chez Monique one last time in her memory.

Monique didn't just love the physical beauty of the place, he said. She felt tied to those who had lived there before. "She thought there was something spiritual."

The family returned to the beach and, after cleaning up after one of the most devastating storms in decades, reopened Chez Monique at the beginning of May. Sandi says Peter was in his element chatting with the hikers. "I've never seen my dad so happy."

Then came June 5, the day Peter drowned.

Hovey says people in Port Renfrew always worried about Peter making that boat trip to Carmanah. The Island's west coast—the Graveyard of the Pacific, the history books call it—is unforgiving. Those supply runs for Chez Monique always came with an element of danger.

On the day it happened, Sandi's husband had already completed the trip in another boat, but by the time Peter arrived the water was too rough. "The waves were absolutely horrifying," Sandi said.

Unable to land, Peter turned back, called out that he would head to Port Renfrew. Then the fog rolled in and they lost him. What happened next is uncertain. Maybe a rogue wave.

When they next saw his boat, it had capsized and was floating toward shore. There was no sign of Peter. Sandi was beside herself. "I searched all over the beach but I couldn't find him." It was the Coast Guard that finally found his body near Carmanah Creek.

Sandi was distraught. "He was my hero, my superman," she said the next day. "He was a very, very wise man." Having lost both Monique and Peter in just five months, her grief was overwhelming.

But she said she intended to keep Chez Monique open. It was home.

a bridge too high

‎———
‎———

IF ANYONE SOUNDED the whistle warning that the Johnson Street Bridge was about to lift, Peter Reitsma didn't hear it.

He was high in the superstructure, burning off old paint and rust with a propane torch. "I was between two panels of steel with the burner going crazy. I didn't hear a thing."

That's how, sixty-five years ago, Reitsma ended up dangling high in the air, hanging on for dear life.

As the saga of Victoria's ninety-four-year-old bridge came to an end in 2018, this is part of the history that few ever knew and fewer still remember.

Reitsma won't forget it, though.

At ninety-one, he's still afraid of heights.

The tale goes back to 1953, the year after Pieter (as he was then known) and Tina Reitsma, married all of two months, left the Netherlands for Victoria.

He took whatever jobs he could, eventually landing with the City of Victoria, which is how he found himself high in the metalwork, preparing the bridge for a new paint job.

There were no safety harnesses in those days. No hard hats, no masks, no cranes or scissor lifts to carry workers aloft. Just grab the blowtorch, clamber up top, and start burning away the old paint.

Every so often, the bridge had to be raised to let ships pass. When that happened, an alarm would sound and the workers would make for a "safe platform"—an immovable part of the span.

Sometimes, Reitsma's location and the noise of the blowtorch would make it impossible to hear the warning, so someone would tug on a gas hose as a signal to come down.

But that didn't happen on the day in question. Reitsma was working at the very top of the bridge when, without warning, it began to move. All he could do was hang on, hoping that it wouldn't open fully.

No such luck. A really tall ship was passing through. The bridge went all the way up.

Reitsma found himself suspended in the air, held by nothing but a metal brace across his lower back. He dropped the still-burning torch.

"The only thing I could do was press myself against the two sides, the plates."

Heaven knows how long he was up there. Fifteen minutes? Twenty? Half an hour? "I cannot say how long it was, but it was a long time."

What did he think of? Nothing.

He was just trying to live—though to this day he firmly believes he had unseen company: "Angels. I'm sure they helped me there. There was no other way I could survive."

When the bridge was finally lowered, Reitsma scrambled down. "I said, 'Why didn't you call me?'" No one had a good answer to that. "The foreman said, 'You can go home.' It was four o'clock anyway."

Reitma's colleagues were surprised when he showed up the next morning. "I've got to work," he said with a shrug. "Got to put bread on the table." They let him toil at ground level after that.

As far as he knows, the incident was never reported. No one even asked how he was. Reitsma moved on to another city job, laying pipe for the water department, then went to work at a Happy Valley Road chicken farm.

Eventually he struck out on his own, first as a carpenter, then a building contractor. Peter Reitsma & Son Construction remains a going concern, though it's the son and grandson running the show now.

As the years passed, the experience on the bridge stayed with Reitsma. On construction sites, he didn't like going on roofs or walking on floor joists. "Still, today, I stay down close to earth," he says.

Reitsma lives in a Saanich house surrounded by his own artwork—handcrafted furniture, beautifully rendered pencil sketches, landscape paintings, examples of traditional decorative art from Hindeloopen, in Friesland.

Friesians are stubborn, he says.

That helped him on the bridge, helped him get a toehold in Canada, helped him when the Germans invaded in the Second World War. When the city of Breda was evacuated, fourteen-year-old Reitsma, carrying his possessions in a couple of pillowcases, came across dead Dutch soldiers on the road, was forced to dive into ditches when the German planes came. During the war he ducked the raids in which young Dutchmen were snatched up for forced labour in Germany.

Then came the day in April 1945 when, perched on a rooftop, he watched Canadian aircraft strafe German positions. Then came the Canadian soldiers in their unfamiliar uniforms, sharing their chocolate bars and cigarettes. Then came his own life in Canada, a good life—though he could have done without that day atop what he still calls "my bridge."

≡

GLADYS SWEETT TURNED 100 on September 6, 2017. Still lived in her own home. Still as goodhearted as her name implied. Still healthy as a somewhat-wobbly-kneed horse. Still sharp as the proverbial.

The news is: that's not news, at least not the way it once was.

It used to be that reaching 100 was a rarity, but now it happens with such frequency that the Queen—herself the nonagenarian daughter of a mother who lived to 101—has had to hire extra staff to handle all the birthday greetings to which her centenarian subjects are entitled.

In fact, the 100-plus crowd is Canada's fastest-growing demographic. The 2016 census showed 8,230 of them, a 41 percent rise in just five years.

Indeed, Gladys is a spring chicken compared to Sooke's Merle Barwis, who was the oldest living Canadian, the fourth longest-lived Canadian ever, and one of the oldest people on the planet when she died in Langford's Priory just a month shy of her 114th birthday in 2014.

It's all part of the well-documented greying of Canada, a shift that has implications for everything from health spending to income tax revenue. We are already at the point where, for the first time, Canada has more seniors than children. Greater Victoria is particularly creaky: it has, relatively speaking, the fewest children of any city in Canada (just 13 percent of the population is under age fifteen) and is top five in seniors (21 percent).

But all those are just numbers. Here's the real story: Gladys Sweett is a treat.

At 100, she is good-humoured and kind, shaped by experiences most of us can only imagine. She has lived through not one but two world wars.

Born Gladys Webb in London, England, in 1917, she was still an infant when the family moved to Calgary, where she grew up. She was an active youngster, liked dancing, even competed at the Highland games ("I came fourth because my piper got drunk"). In fact, it was at Penley's dance hall that she met her husband, back in the days when the guys literally filled out the girls' dance cards. "He would say, 'There's not room for my name' and he would cross everybody else's out."

She married Eddie (he went by his second name because his mother had given all her sons the same first name, Albert) in June 1939, then lost him to the army when the Second World War broke out that September.

He was gone six years.

Eddie escaped Juno Beach unscathed on D-Day, only to be wounded later. Gladys didn't hear a word for a long time. Then one day the postman came running down the street waving a postcard saying Eddie was coming home.

That's when the marriage really began, when they had their three kids. Eventually, Eddie's job with the CPR brought the family to Victoria, where he toiled on the E&N and Gladys worked for Kmart.

They were married fifty-seven years before he died. "I wish he were here to celebrate with me," she said on her 100th birthday. She still lives in the house they built in 1966.

Bowling was a passion for both of them. (In fact, Gladys made the pages of the *Times Colonist* when she protested the closing of the Town and Country lanes in 2005.) She figures organizing the bowling leagues, working out the stats, kept her mind sharp.

She emails and Skypes on her computer, gets a physical workout at Luther Court, does the newspaper puzzles for mental gymnastics.

She is also invested in the world around her, reads the newspaper cover to cover, watches the news, votes Green. Turned down a dinner invitation from daughter Bev Knapton in 2016 because she didn't want to miss the Hillary–Trump debate. Has no use for the US president. ("I hope I live long enough to see what happens to him," she said.)

Not that she plans to go anywhere soon, though. Note that she just got a new rescue dog, Maggie.

That's the difference today. Turning 100 doesn't mean turning off a switch. It's not a signal to fade away. Kirk Douglas used his 100th birthday as an opportunity to pen an open letter ripping Trump. Another screen icon, *Gone with the Wind*'s Olivia de Havilland, 101, recently sued FX Networks over the way she was portrayed in the TV series *Feud*—an action that showed faith in a) her own longevity and b) the speed of the American legal system. (BTW, de Havilland's father, Walter, lived in Victoria, where he was known as a chess player, in the 1940s and '50s. It was there that he met his third wife, Rosemary Beaton Connor, who died in 2005 at age 101.)

Gladys's advice?

Eat healthily. Stay active. Stay positive. Don't get dragged down worrying about things beyond your control. Also, a small rye and Seven helps.

As Greater Victoria's newest centenarian—a 160-member club in a region of 377,000—she is content.

"I've had a good life, a very good life."

the last word

EDDY ZZYLINSKI IS dead. I killed him.

Sure, they'll say he died of exposure, but who do you think pulled back the covers under which he was sheltering?

Zzylinski lived in the phone book, on the very last line of the Victoria listings. He first appeared in the Telus SuperPages in 2001, though he was known as Zyylinsky—one z, three y's—back then. After that he went by Zylinski before the appearance of Zza's Pizzeria in 2004 forced him to add the extra z to ensure that he kept that precious last spot in the directory.

Yes, Dear Reader, Eddy turned out to be a cheerful fake.

No kidding. For a few years in the 2000s, the last name in the Victoria directory was a fiction created for the sole purpose of occupying the last line in the listings. He existed only in the fertile imagination of a fellow named B.B. Bernamoff.

The obvious question is: Why? To which the answer is: For fun. Which, when you think about it, is as good a reason as any. Bernamoff—at least, we think that's his name—figured being dead last has its advantages, or at least did in the pre-girlfriend days. Meet someone in a bar and you can say, "If you want to call me, ring the last name in the phone book." But mostly he just did it for fun.

When we met him in 2005, Bernamoff was forty-nine, had been retired from the restaurant business since age thirty-five.

"Now I hustle a little poker on the side—online poker—to make ends meet," he said. For some reason, the image of Kramer from *Seinfeld* came to mind. He had got the last-listing idea from a Las Vegas newspaper story twenty years before, but acted on it only after moving to Victoria from Calgary in the 1990s.

"It was on my list of things to do in my life. It kind of goes along with paragliding. This is just easier than paragliding."

Getting Eddy into the phone book wasn't hard. For an extra $1.80 a month, the phone folks were happy to provide separate listings to roommates sharing the same number.

As mentioned, B.B.'s "roommate" was first known as Eddy Zyylinsky. The name just popped out of his mouth.

But uh-oh, it wasn't long before Zza's Pizzeria opened, bumping Eddy up a notch in the phone book. So Telus was told there should be two *z*'s in Zzylinsky. Sorry, said the phone company, and added the extra letter.

By chance, Zyylinsky, or Zzylinski, or Bernamoff, or whatever his name is, knew the big cheese at Zza's and announced his intention to outlast the pizzeria in the race for the bottom. "I told him 'I will go to the mat with you. Next year it will be three *z*'s, then four *z*'s.'"

Zza's, as befits this story, then changed its name to something completely different.

Really, says B.B., this last-name business is just a lark, one of those goofy things that guys do because they're guys.

"This is why women divorce men. We're immature . . . We have a higher desire to have fun."

Um, are you divorced, B.B.?

Yes, he allowed that he was, but added that he and the ex got along famously.

He also noted that this was not the first time he had played the name game. He had actually changed his legally ten years earlier, switching from Brian to B.B.—which is what everyone called him anyway. (When people asked how he got the handle, he would tell them his great-great-grandfather was the inventor of the BB gun. "Really?" they would invariably ask. "No, not really," he would reply.)

He was also toying with the idea of changing his name again: once, after hearing a man on a Florida street holler out "Hey, Charlie!"—the way the guy said it, it rhymed with Sally—Bernamoff vowed he would change his first name to Chally to celebrate his fiftieth birthday. (Alas, when the time came around, he decided it would be too much hassle, so decided to learn how to dance—you know, salsa, ballroom—instead. "I've always been a klutzy guy, so I said if I don't go through with changing my name, then I'll take dancing to punish myself.")

The thing is, Zzylinskigate came to light only because Bernamoff decided not to hang me out to dry. After I called him up while researching a piece on the 2005 phone book, he and his buddies toyed with the idea of inventing a fantastic history for Eddy Zzylinski—something about ditching the astronaut program for life as a professional poker player in Vegas—but decided it wouldn't be right to let me put my name on a lie. His was an honourable confession, uncoerced. For this, I was grateful.

As for the phone book people, they didn't really know what to do other than giggle. SuperPages' Jules Heyward said he had never heard of anything like the Zzylinski yarn. They often contended with name-changing businesses clawing their way to the top of the A list (in Los Angeles, Aadlen

Brothers Auto Wrecking, the junkyard that appeared in countless Hollywood movies, added a second *a* for that purpose) but never to the back of the book.

Except when the next phone book came out in 2006, it was sans Zzylinski, much to the chagrin of his creator. "They took my alias away, the bastards," fumed Bernamoff. No warning at all. The Zzylinski listing just disappeared, poof, like Arsenio Hall.

The guy who replaced Zzylinski with the new last listing in Victoria said he would be just as happy to give up the title. Len Zywicki had had it before, and said it just brought out the cranks. "I did get a call, two in the morning, as soon as the new book came out."

Being at the back of the alphabet does have some minor advantages, Zywicki said. When you know yours will be the last name called, you can plan a nap or bring out a book. On election day, you automatically go to the farthest table and tell the clerks, "I'm the last name on your list."

There was some muttering about bringing Zzylinski back to life in the manner of Frankenstein's monster, but that didn't happen. Last I heard, a couple of years ago, Bernamoff was still Bernamoff, driving a cab in Victoria. Eddy Zzylinski had gone the way of the phone book itself.

The directory, whose annual arrival used to be anticipated as eagerly as the next *Star Wars* movie, has all but vanished from the typical home or office. Ottawa says copies of directories must be available on request, but who requests them anymore? Cell phones aren't listed, and the type has shrunk to a size normally reserved for the bottom of insurance policies and car rental agreements. In Victoria, a city in which optometrists use only the top three lines of the eye chart, that's a problem.

Also, the phone book isn't as much fun without Eddy. So, to thank him for being straight with me, I'll give him the honour of the last line in this book instead.

Cheers, Eddy Zzylinski.

acknowledgements

PEOPLE TRUST ME with their stories. They take a deep breath and hope that I not only will get the facts right and quote them accurately but, more importantly, will use those facts and quotes in a way that reflects who they are and how they feel.

After forty years in newspapers, I sometimes take this for granted. I shouldn't. It's a big deal to let a stranger enter your life and package you up for public consumption, particularly when that stranger has been granted access to a larger audience than most people will ever have.

So, with that in mind, I first have to thank the people— thousands of them—who have entrusted me with their tales.

I wish I could have included more of them in this book. They include a man who, after working all his life, found himself living in his car, using an upturned golf club as a cane to hobble around on the bad feet that had cost him his job; a man who crouched in the back of a pickup, stopping Wayne Gretzky from tumbling out of it on live TV while heading to light the Olympic cauldron; a cop who was robbed at gunpoint by other cops while on United Nations duty; the Heroes of Hartley Bay who rushed to the rescue when the *Queen of the North* sank; a Victoria physician who opened a brothel in New

Zealand; a guy who collected banana slugs for a living; a guy who gutted it out to a last-place finish in the Tour de France; the seemingly indestructible Mike Lawless who, after years of volunteering for the Cops for Cancer Tour de Rock, saw the irony in himself dying too young of cancer; all the cancer-stricken Tour kids and their families, whose raw humanity humbled me. I could go on and on, but I won't. Lucky you.

I will take a moment to thank a few people, including my colleagues at the Victoria *Times Colonist*. Among them are the editor-in-chief, Dave Obee (who co-authored the piece on Richard Reiter), a long list of copy editors who died a little bit every time they handled one of my stories, and the photographers—Debra Brash, Adrian Lam, Ray Smith, Lyle Stafford, Darren Stone, Bruce Stotesbury—whose work appears here. Debra, with whom I go way back (she, her husband, my wife, and I were all in the same how-to-get-married class in 1983), deserves special mention; she was my partner in exploring the backroads and unearthing many of the stories you just read.

The people at Heritage House were as wonderful as always: Pat and Rodger Touchie, Lara Kordic, Leslie Kenny, Lenore Hietkamp, John Walls. Merrie-Ellen Wilcox proved a meticulous editor, saving you, dear reader, from my brain cramps. Jacqui Thomas designed yet another clever and compelling cover.

Most of all, I have to thank my lovely and long-suffering wife, Lucille. Sorry, dear.

index

Murmansk, 108
MV *Coho*, 178

Nagasaki, 78–84, 86–87
'Namgis First Nation, 146
National Museum of Man.
    See Canadian Museum of History.
National Museum of the American
    Indian (Smithsonian), 147–48,
    149
native languages, 4, 6–7, 27–41.
    See also by name.
Nguyen, Hiep, 65–67, 69
9/11, 180, 181, 182
Nootka Island, 4, 27, 28
Nootka Trail, 8, 9
Normandy. *See* D-Day.
Nuchatlaht language, 27, 28, 29,
    37, 38
Nuu-chah-nulth language, 29,
    36, 37
Nuyumbalees Cultural Centre, 148

Obee, Dave, 14–15, 16
Oclucje, 28
Oldfield Orchard, 141, 142
Olive Odyssey, 60–61
100-plus demographic, 194,
    196–97
*On Island: Life Among the Coast
    Dwellers* (book), 177
Orchard on View, 140, 141–42

Parlow, Bob, 96
Paterson, Dave, 97, 98
Pender Island, 168–71
Pho Vy Vietnamese Restaurant,
    65, 67
plastic garbage, 76–77
Poole, Frank, 96
Port Angeles, 178–79
potlatches, 33, 146–47, 148, 153

Prince Henry (ship), 97–98, 99, 105
Prince David (ship), 99
prisoners of war, 78–84, 87,
    90–91, 96, 100, 107–8, 113–15,
    118–19, 165
prisons, 49, 50–52, 53–55
property crime, 49, 50, 51, 52

Qualicum, 143, 144

Ramsay, Peter, 96
Rankin, Murray, 165
RCMP, 47. *See also* Beckett, Sarah.
Ready for the Fray (book), 96,
    99, 100
Reddish, Iain, 11–13
Reiter, Günter, 14, 15, 16, 19
Reiter, Karl, 15, 16
Reiter, Maria (Mitzi), 14, 15, 16, 18
Reiter, Richard, 14–22
Reitsma, Peter, 191–93
Reitsma, Tina, 191
Remington, Bob, 154, 156
residential schools, 7, 28, 31, 33,
    147, 148, 185, 186
Ressam, Ahmed, 178–80, 182
Robinson, Dave, 47, 48
Robinson, Ken, 46–48
roller skating, 23–26
Ross, Stew, 97
Rowboat in a Hurricane (book), 59
Roy, Reg, 96, 99, 100
Royal Canadian Air Force, 107, 113
Royal Hamilton Light Infantry, 119
Royal Ontario Museum, 147, 148
Royal Regiment of Canada, 106–7
Royal Winnipeg Rifles, 97, 98, 104
Russell, Hector, 101–2

Salishan languages, 29–30
Salt Spring Island, 101, 103, 120
Sam, Ian, 40
same-sex marriage, 123–24

about the author

JACK KNOX IS the author of two bestselling humour books, *Hard Knox: Musings from the Edge of Canada* and *Opportunity Knox: Twenty Years of Award-Losing Humour Writing*, both based on his popular column at the Victoria *Times Colonist* and both long-listed for the Leacock Medal for Humour. Knox's career highlights include being blasted with blowhole spray by Luna the orca whale, interviewing a nude porn star, and getting a phone call from Barack Obama four days before the 2008 presidential election. In his spare time he performs in a rock 'n' roll band with members of his Tour de Rock cycling team.